Stripping and Finishing

in a weekend

Jane Davies

MEREHURST

Cast iron fireplace (page 40)

Contents

Garden bench (page 44)

Gilded mirror (page 56)

Ladder back chair (page 66)

Introduction

Interior design trends change with alarming speed, mirroring the fashion world with new shapes, colours and global influences. However, most affordable furniture is mass-produced and machine-finished to keep up with these trends, offering little scope for individuality. As we are encouraged to renew and replace, many items of furniture are consigned to the rubbish dump with years of life left in them, all they really need is for someone to look at them with new eyes and spot their potential.

Mastering the techniques of stripping and re-finishing will help you tap into that potential, whether you are a skilled enthusiast or an absolute beginner. There is nothing more satisfying than putting a stamp of individuality on your home and knowing that the unique look that you have created cannot be bought on the high street.

Ordinary items of furniture that have survived several generations of use acquire their own, unique patina of age; they also tend to be better quality than their modern equivalents as they were expected to last a lifetime, if not several generations. This meant that stripping and re-finishing became an essential skill rather than a creative hobby. I hope that the basic techniques of stripping and finishing set out in this book will inspire you to preserve and enhance these qualities. They should also give you the confidence to adapt and change items to suit your lifestyle.

Specialist finishing materials are now widely available and some of the labour-intensive finishes are giving way to a softer, more colourful approach where rules are made to be broken. Many modern decorating products are both easier to use and to dispose of. Oil- and solvent-based paints and varnishes are rapidly being replaced with less toxic water-based alternatives. You only need to visit a DIY store to be bombarded with choices of colours and finishes.

In the projects that follow, I have tried to cover a broad cross-section of traditional and more contemporary finishes. However, as the possibilities are endless a techniques section is also included, which will help you to identify the material you are working on and recommend the most efficient methods of stripping and preparation before choosing a suitable finish.

Once you have acquired a piece of furniture you need to identify the existing finish. This is often difficult because many different finishes may have been applied over the years. For an at-a-glance summary of the different stripping methods and their suitability, refer to the table on page 13. Before committing to a new finish, spend some time testing different methods and colourways on scraps of wood or metal. This will also help you master different techniques as well as preventing time-consuming mistakes. Remember that the item should be finished

to suit the purpose for which it is used, for example, a coffee table will need a protective barrier from water marks and everyday wear and tear.

Furniture restoration has traditionally been associated with quality antiques; however, I have chosen a selection of readily available and affordable junk shop finds. I believe that this demonstrates what it is possible to achieve with the humblest of items. If you are a beginner, start on a small item as preparation can often take longer than anticipated; the real reward is standing back and admiring your finished piece. Work your way up to larger and more ambitious projects as your confidence grows – each project can be adapted to suit your own style. Once bitten by the restoring bug I guarantee you will find it impossible to pass a junk shop without having a glance inside.

Jane Davies

Inspirations

Interior styles are constantly evolving with exciting new colours, textures and shapes. Learning how to absorb all this information will allow you to choose a finish for furniture and fittings that reflects your individual style.

When placed in the right setting a carefully restored item of furniture or architectural fitting will give your home a highly individual style, which will far outlive the latest interior fashion trend. The main aim of this book is to help you identify suitable candidates for restoration and apply the appropriate stripping and re-finishing technique within a weekend. It is important to learn to trust your own instincts when selecting items to work on: the first rule is to choose items that you like (even if you don't know why!) as you can often feel inspired by an object's shape, colour, texture or material. Be realistic about the condition of the item and, remember that a bargain is not a bargain if it falls apart before you get it home.

Before setting out on a furniture hunt, it is helpful to note down the dimensions of the rooms you hope to buy pieces for, including the room heights, and any niches and alcoves. Seasoned furniture restorers will probably carry these and a tape measure with them at all times. It is particularly important to have accurate measurements of the front door and stairwell – you do not want to end up sawing your precious find in half to get it up the stairs.

Assessing the item

Stripping and restoring fixtures and furniture is a bit of a lottery, but the biggest challenge is to re-finish and adapt the item to fit in with your existing decor and lifestyle.

Complementary styles

If you are lucky enough to have beautiful period features in your home, carefully stripping and re-finishing them will maintain their good looks for years to come. Even if you do not wish to recreate the traditional style, original shutters or a solid wooden fire surround add character and warmth to any scheme. Quality materials, such as hardwoods and intricate cast iron often dictate their own finishes, requiring nothing more elaborate than a clear finish to let the surface colour and texture shine through.

Older items, which have mellowed with the years, acquire their own patina of age and can look too shiny and new if over-restored. If you are adding contemporary items to a period interior, it is worth considering finishes that give an 'antiqued' effect, so that they blend in comfortably with their surroundings.

Record your ideas

Style books and magazines are a great source of ideas, and museums with collections of furniture provide a rich source of inspiration. Holidays abroad also open your eyes to different colours, designs and textures, from cool Scandinavian colours on blond woods to African earth shades on exotic hardwoods.

Although conventional places are always a good starting point, colour ideas can come from sources as diverse as a metallic finish on a car to a leaf picked up in a park. The idea for the simple flower motif on this changing screen (left) may well have come from a spring-flowering garden.

Start a scrapbook of pictures that appeal to you and experiment with different materials to recreate them: you will soon discover your style. Do not be afraid to change the use of a piece of furniture completely and to mix and match different styles and materials until you achieve the effect you are looking for.

Gone are the days when unwanted pieces of furniture are consigned to the nearest skip, although it is still worth looking in them on the off chance. The cheapest source of furniture is friends and relatives – most people have a few items stashed in the attic or garage that they would be only too happy to give away.

When you have exhausted this supply, try junk shops, furniture auctions, car boot sales and adverts in local newspapers. Junk shops that specialize in house clearances can be a real treasure trove and the best bargains are often to be had in the least fashionable areas. Furniture auctions can be useful if you are looking for a particular item and time is limited because you can request a catalogue by post before attending the auction. But remember that the auction house will add their commission onto the successful bid and they can only provide an estimate of the price an item is expected fetch. You will also find furniture at the larger car boot fairs, although many sellers are actually antique dealers rather than ordinary members of the public. The small ads in local newspapers are also worth looking at, but the vendor's description can often be wide of the mark. If an item sounds interesting, ring up first and get a detailed description, which includes the size, before making a special journey to see the piece.

Prices will also reflect interior trends, for example, retro styles from the 1950's and 1960's are currently very popular, which means that items you could not give away a few years ago have jumped in value and are set to become the antiques of the future. It is worth doing a little research into the history of furniture and interior design as this will help you develop a good eye for shape and detail. Once you have identified the approximate age of a piece of furniture from its shape and form, you can make an informed guess as to the material it is made from, even if the original finish is obscured.

Quick changes

One of the quickest ways to transform a room is to change the accessories, as these often emphasize the style. Smaller items such as lamp bases, picture frames, candlesticks, and occasional tables are ideal projects to start with if you want to try out a re-finishing technique. They are quick to complete and will build your confidence and expertise before tackling larger pieces. Small items are also ideal for more adventurous finishes because they add 'accent' colours (strongly contrasting detail) to a room but will not over-dominate it.

Selecting a finish

When it comes to deciding on a finished style, personal taste is paramount. Most contemporary finishes have their roots in ancient techniques. Over the centuries, styles have been borrowed from all over the world and been adapted as tastes changed. Many labour-intensive finishes, such as traditional oriental lacquerwork, which used up to one hundred layers of carefully applied varnish, can be replicated with simpler materials and methods.

Techniques traditionally employed to trick the eye and suggest wealth, such as faux marble, woodgraining and stone effects are now recognized for their own merit. Expensive gold leaf that would once have been painstakingly applied with water gilding techniques can now be replicated with much cheaper Dutch metal leaf applied to gold size.

Identifying the finish and the material

Before you begin, it is important to identify the finish you are dealing with so that you can apply the most effective stripping method. This is the one that will do the least damage to the surface. If in doubt, carry out a test patch on an area of the item that will remain hidden.

TRANSLUCENT AND CLEAR FINISHES ON WOOD

Translucent finishes tend to be the more traditional method of finishing wooden furniture and fixtures, and are usually used on pieces made from good quality wood as they enhance the lustre and colour of the wood without hiding the pattern of the grain. It is also possible to use stains and dyes to make softwoods (which are usually pale) imitate the richer colours of more expensive hardwoods.

The more traditional methods of finishing wood are known as 'soft finishes' and require great care, skill, time and patience to master. French polishing is the most difficult technique of all; it comes in the form of bleached white polish for pale woods as well as the more traditional colours. For a completely natural look, many people

GILT CREAM OVER RED EMULSION

SILVER TRANSFER LEAF IN BLUE EMULSION

BLUE METALLIC SPRAY PAINT

BLUE WAX OVER WHITE EMULSION

SATIN COLOURED VARNISH

COLOURED WOODSTAIN

DRIFTWOOD WOOD WASH

TEAK WOODSTAIN

choose wax, which nourishes the wood and can be buffed to a rich sheen. However, this is a delicate finish, which is easily marked by water and heat: to overcome this, the piece can be varnished first, then waxed to soften the effect. An oiled finish is water-resistant, although it will darken the colour of the wood.

Modern acrylic or polyurethane varnish is the toughest of the finishes providing a water-repellent surface. It is available in gloss, satin or matt and may come completely transparent or tinted in a huge variety of colours. Dye and stain are sold separately and will change the colour of the wood requiring a protective coat of varnish or wax. Relatively new to the market are wood washes, which provide a translucent veil of colour and a matt varnish in one.

For all the finishes, a test patch is recommended to identify the finish. This is best carried out in an area that will not be seen, for example under a tabletop. Start with a piece of wire wool dipped in white spirit; if this has no effect, try methylated spirit and finally resort to paint/varnish stripper.

WAXED OR OILED FINISHES

A waxed finish can normally be identified by touch; the surface of the piece will feel warm and waxy, and it may smell of beeswax and have a satin finish. An oiled finish will have a more subtle sheen making it harder to identify easily.

SHELLAC/FRENCH POLISH-BASED FINISHES

These are traditional antique finishes that usually give the surface of the item a rich colour and highly polished, mirror-like sheen. Another recognizable characteristic is that it is an easily damaged finish that may have scratch marks, water stains and ring marks marring the surface.

SHELLAC BUTTON POLISH

LIMING WAX ON HARDWOOD

LIGHT OAK SATIN VARNISH

LIMING WAX ON SOFTWOOD

GLOSS POLYURETHENE VARNISH ON HARDWOOD

OILED FINISH ON HARDWOOD

OILED FINISH ON SOFTWOOD

GLOSS POLYURETHENE VARNISH ON SOFTWOOD

OPAQUE FINISHES ON WOOD

These are finishes that disguise the surface material, as well as adding colour to the finish. Oil-based paints offer the greatest protection providing a tough, durable finish. Whereas water-based paints require varnishing or waxing when used on furniture.

OIL-BASED PAINT ON WOOD

Oil-based paint, which is known under a variety of names such as gloss, satinwood and eggshell gives a tough durable finish generally used in areas of high wear and tear, and it can usually be recognized by its shiny, light-reflective appearance. It is a practical finish, which can be washed clean and is used on most architectural woodwork including doors, skirting boards and architraves.

The brittle nature of oil-based paint makes it one of the easiest finishes to remove; there are several techniques that can be used successfully. In order to minimize surface damage, select the least drastic method possible.

WATER-BASED PAINT ON WOOD

Water-based paints and tinted glazes are often used in hand-painted finishes and paint effects such as stencilling, dragging and marbling on furniture, doors and other architectural woodwork. Water-based finishes will almost always have had an additional coat of varnish or wax to protect the surface so this will need to be removed as well as the paint below. If the piece has been waxed after painting the surface will feel waxy to the touch – use the method described on page 24 to remove the wax before tackling the painted surface. If the item has been varnished it is likely that a water-based acrylic varnish has been used. This can be stripped using conventional liquid paint stripper.

BLACK GLOSS

CRACKLE GLAZE WITH EMULSION

MATT EMULSION

OIL-BASED EGGSHELL

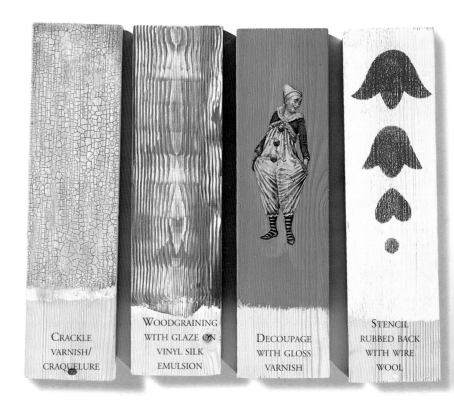

CRACKLE VARNISH/ CRAQUELURE

WOODGRAINING WITH GLAZE ON VINYL SILK EMULSION

DECOUPAGE WITH GLOSS VARNISH

STENCIL RUBBED BACK WITH WIRE WOOL

Special cases

These are items that have the usual range of finishes but will require special stripping techniques.

ENAMELLED FINISHES ON METAL
The enamelling process actually bonds the finish chemically to the metal. One of the only effective methods of removing it would be to have the item professionally sandblasted; a method that can also be used for painted metal.

METAL FURNITURE AND ARCHITECTURAL METALWORK
Most metal surfaces are painted or finished with an oil-based paint, which protects against rust, corrosion and tarnishing. Metallic fixtures around the home need to be maintained and protected with specialist finishes that suit the job they must perform. For example, radiators, hot water pipes, metal stoves and barbecues should be coated with paint that can withstand high temperatures. Ordinary paint used on these items will yellow quickly. Many items of furniture, such as wrought iron beds have been finished with enamel paint or lacquer, which adheres best to super-smooth surfaces.

CANE/WICKER, RATTAN AND PAPER
Once these items have been painted they are extremely difficult to strip because the crevices within the intricately woven material become embedded with paint. It is also important to note that, while cane, wicker and rattan can be safely stripped with paint stripper, extreme care should be taken with Lloyd Loom furniture. The manufacturing technique used to make this type of furniture involves twisting strands of paper around a wire core, which was then woven to produce its distinctive style. This type of furniture should not be stripped back to the bare material. If you wish to re-finish one of these items, brushing away flaking paint and lightly sanding with fine grade abrasive paper is sufficient preparation.

FLOORBOARDS
Floorboards are a special case unless they are in good condition. The most efficient way of stripping a floor back to bare wood is to hire an industrial floor sander, which will remove the top surface of the boards ready to be finished. You will also need an edging sander to get into awkward corners.

VENEERS AND MARQUETRY
Great care must be taken when stripping furniture with these thin wooden inlays. Veneers and marquetry are made of thin slivers of wood, which are glued and bonded in place with heat. Avoid applying water to the surface as this will cause the wood to swell and buckle. Soft finishes should be carefully stripped with white spirit or a preparatory soft finish remover.

MELAMINE
This is synthetic, man-made material widely used in fitted furniture manufacturing as it is easy to clean and maintain, although it can often look dull and clinical. For this reason, it is now possible to buy specialized products that make it easy to re-finish the shiny surface. Stripping is not applicable to melamine, it should be lightly sanded with fine grade abrasive paper, which will key the surface allowing the paint to adhere. A special primer should then be applied to provide a smooth matt base for the final paint colour. When finishing melamine, a hard-wearing satinwood or gloss paint should be used to provide a tough surface.

TILES
Tiles are also a special case, although they cannot be stripped. Instead they can be re-finished using tile primer and tile paint, which has been formulated to withstand cleaning. Apply tile primer with a sponge roller to avoid visible brush marks and obscure any unwanted pattern. Special gloss paint can then be applied with a brush or foam roller in solid blocks of colour, or applied in patterns.

PROFESSIONAL STRIPPING METHODS

Although fast and effective, these methods can ruin an item if used inappropriately. Always choose a reputable outlet and ask to see items that they have recently stripped.

CAUSTIC DIPPING
One of the quickest methods of stripping any finish on wood is by caustic dipping. This is definitely not a DIY job; look in the phone book to find your nearest outlet. Dipping is a very harsh method, which should only be attempted if it is impossible to use other stripping methods, or if you have a large number of doors or banister spindles to strip. The drawbacks of caustic dipping are that it can dissolve glued joints, warp the wood and give the item a bleached appearance, although this can be corrected to a certain extent with wood restorer.

SANDBLASTING
This is another method that cannot be attempted at home. It is usually used to strip paint from metal and masonry. The technique involves particles of sand being fired at the item at a high velocity to strip away the surface. It is not suitable for use on delicate items but is useful for large areas. It is often used to clean dirt and pollution damage from the exterior of buildings.

Stripping the finish

Before applying a new finish, you will need to strip away the existing old finish, especially if it is in poor state of repair. Time taken at this stage will reveal the true condition of the item underneath and allow repairs to be made.

STRIPPING WITH A HOT-AIR GUN

SUITABILITY: stripping oil-based paints and varnish on wood and metal. They are widely available to buy or hire; the most effective models have variable temperature settings and come with a scraper attachment, enabling you to use the tool with one hand and leaving the other hand free. Because the gun rapidly heats up the paint, perform a test patch to gauge the length of time the heat should be applied.

ADVANTAGES: speed and cleanliness. Cost-effective method over large areas, such as doors .

DISADVANTAGES: care must be taken near glass and there is a high risk of scorching the wood. Expensive if you only have one item to strip. Floors should be protected and singed paint swept up and disposed of carefully once cool.

1 Turn on the heat gun pointing it away from the painted surface. After a few seconds, hold the gun with the integral scraper blade resting against

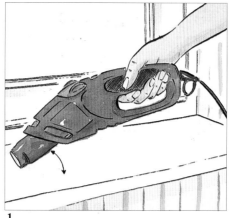

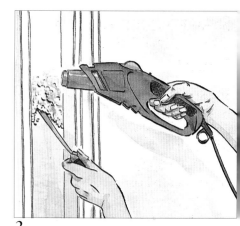

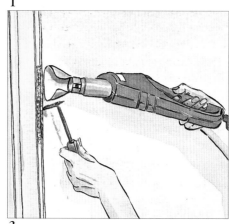

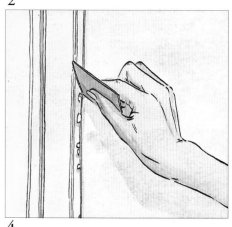

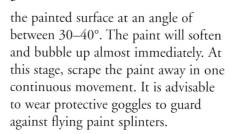

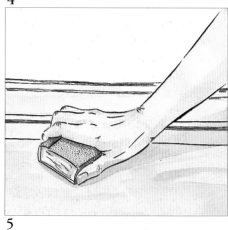

the painted surface at an angle of between 30–40°. The paint will soften and bubble up almost immediately. At this stage, scrape the paint away in one continuous movement. It is advisable to wear protective goggles to guard against flying paint splinters.

2 When stripping vertical areas, scrape downwards or horizontally to prevent the stripped paint falling down into the gun and igniting. Work in small sections scraping away the soft paint immediately; if the section is too large the paint will re-harden.

3 For part-glazed items, such as doors, use a glass protector nozzle. Fitted to the end of the gun, it deflects the heat away from the glass and prevents it from cracking. Hold the heat gun with the nozzle next to the glass surface, and remove the nearby paint with a hand-held scraper.

4 Remove any remaining paint with liquid paint stripper, applied with fine grade wire wool. Paint stuck in beading or moulding can often be 'pinged' off using the pointed end of a paint scraper blade or cabinet scraper.

5 After stripping, sand the surface thoroughly with a fine grade abrasive paper wrapped around a sanding block or attached to an electric sander.

STRIPPING WITH A LIQUID JELLY PAINT/VARNISH STRIPPER

SUITABILITY: all types of paint, varnish, lacquer and shellac-based finishes, although equally effective on wood and metal.

ADVANTAGES: a quick, effective method on one to three coats. Works well on detailed mouldings as the jelly can penetrate the nooks and crannies. Most effective on horizontal surfaces. New formulations of liquid stripper do not contain methylene chloride or methanol. This makes them 'low odour' and more pleasant to use.

DISADVANTAGES: will need to be reapplied on heavily over-painted items. This is an efficient, if slightly messy, technique so make sure the floor surface is well protected. The liquid jelly consistency can run off vertical surfaces. Relatively expensive if you have large areas to strip.

1 Make sure that the surface of the item is clean and free from dust. Pour some of the stripper into a glass or metal container (it will melt some plastics) and use an old paintbrush to apply a thick layer of stripper to the item. Do not over-brush the area once the stripper has been applied.

If stripping paint, allow the stripper to penetrate all the layers. The surface of the paint will quickly begin to blister and wrinkle. Test with a paint scaper to see if the paint comes away easily.

2 If stripping varnish or shellac, do not leave the stripper sitting on the surface; remove with wire wool or a paint scraper as soon as it is applied. The finish should dissolve easily revealing bare wood.

3 Use a paint scraper to remove some of the paint/stripper mixture, scrape it away gently and if bare wood is revealed continue removing. If another layer of paint is revealed beneath leave the stripper for longer, or if it appears to have stopped working remove the paint/stripper mixture and apply a fresh coat of stripper. Continue the process until all the paint is removed.

4 Use a nylon-bristled toothbrush to work the stripper into awkward crevices. Any remaining traces of paint can be removed by scrubbing with wire wool dipped in paint remover. Once the wire wool becomes clogged up with paint, dispose of it carefully and begin again with a fresh piece.

5 When the entire painted finish is stripped, neutralize the item by wiping thoroughly with water or white spirit (water will raise the grain of wood more than white spirit but white spirit may react with water-based finishes).

Hints and Tips

The chemicals within the stripper are very powerful, so wear heavy-duty gloves and keep your arms and legs covered to protect against accidental splashes. Carefully dispose of used wire wool and paint stripper by wrapping it up in several layers of newspaper.

1

2

3

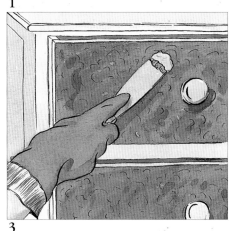

4

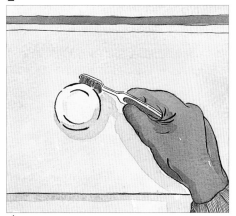

5

STRIPPING WITH A PASTE STRIPPER

SUITABILITY: a fairly clean method for stripping wood and metal items. Working times will vary, so always follow manufacturers' instructions.
ADVANTAGES: its thick consistency enables it to cling to vertical and overhead surfaces, as well as covering intricate shapes.
DISADVANTAGES: needs to be washed off/neutralized with water, which makes it unsuitable for veneered items. It can slightly darken the colour of wood and can be fairly tricky to apply evenly to awkard shapes.

1 The item must be clean and dust free. Apply the paste using a trowel or paint scraper to the manufacturers' recommended thickness, pushing it into any crevices. Leave for at least 15 minutes before lifting away a small test section. If the paint is not coming

1

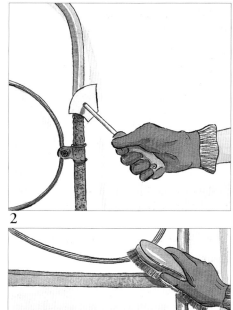

2

3

away easily, spread the paste back over the area. Make regular checks until the paste is ready to be removed.

2 Peel the paste gently away from the item with the aid of a paint scraper. If necessary reapply paste to stubborn areas of paint.

3 Scrub the item well with water and a stiff brush. Give it a final rinse with clean water to remove any residue.

STRIPPING WITH A PEEL-AWAY BLANKET STRIPPER

SUITABILITY: an excellent method for wooden, metal, brick and stone surfaces that have been over-painted many times. Because it is neutralized with water it is not suitable for use on veneered surfaces. Fairly expensive to use over a large area.
ADVANTAGES: removes paint cleanly leaving very little residue. Needs virtually no scraping, which makes it a good choice for delicate or easily scratched surfaces. Once applied, simply wait for the paint to solidify onto the blanket, then lift away.
DISADVANTAGES: it can take several hours to work and is slightly messy to remove. It can be tricky to use on vertical and shaped surfaces because it

1

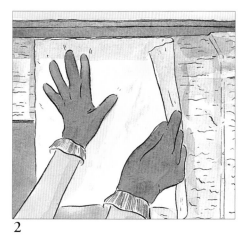

2

is important that the blanket makes contact with all areas of the paste. It will sometimes need to be cut to fit large, bulky or awkward shaped items. On some porous surfaces, peel-away blanket stripper needs to be neutralized with a special solution, which should be supplied with it.

1 Use the plastic spatula supplied in the pack to spread the paste thickly over the item pressing it firmly into any carvings or crevices.

2 Unfold the polythene and tissue blanket and place it laminated side down over the item. Starting in the

centre, press the paper firmly against the paste with both hands and smooth away any trapped air bubbles. Leave for at least one hour before performing a test patch.

3 Peel back a small area of the polythene and tissue blanket. If the paint has solidified onto the paste (known as saponification) and the bare surface of the item is visible, the entire cover can be carefully removed. If it has not solidified, add more paste to the area, re-cover and wait another hour. Repeat the above process until the bare surface of the item appears beneath the paint and stripper.

4 Carefully peel back the polythene and tissue blanket. Lumps of stripper and old paint will be stuck to the surface; other bits should be fairly solid

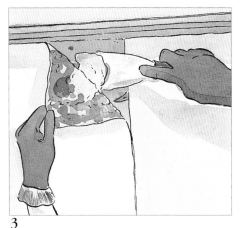

3

and can be removed with a stripping knife. Once all the stripper has been removed, wash the piece thoroughly with clean running water (outside with a hose pipe is ideal; if this is not possible stand the piece in a bath or sink). The paste is supplied with a pH testing kit and a neutralizing solution that should be applied if necessary.

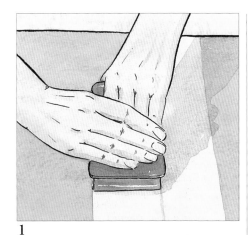

4

Hints and Tips

This method is recommended for historial buildings and restoration projects where damage to the surface must be avoided. Apply it to ceilings with delicate plaster mouldings using a roller.

STRIPPING WITH A CABINET SCRAPER

SUITABILITY: gloss paint and most varnished finishes on wooden surfaces.
ADVANTAGES: the cheapest stripping method. Removes paint and polishes the wood beneath. Works well on awkward areas such as glazing bars and beading. Good as a finishing technique used with another stripping method.
DISADVANTAGES: time-consuming and tricky to use as it needs constant pressure making it hard on the hands. The rolled steel blade needs to be kept sharp if it is to work properly.

1 Position scraper at a 70°-angle to the surface and pull firmly towards you until the paint begins to flake away.

2 Continue the process until all the paint is removed. If the blade becomes blunt and ineffective follow the manufacturers' sharpening technique.

1

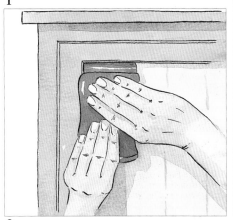

2

STRIPPING WITH AN ELECTRIC SANDER

SUITABILITY: works well on painted and varnished wooden surfaces that are to be re-painted. The multi-functional sanders are particularly useful as they combine different shaped bases for orbital sanding, as well as different shaped profiles for sanding a variety of shapes including spindles and mouldings. Most electric sanders have variable speed settings and their instruction manuals will advise on the speed to use for different surfaces.
ADVANTAGES: a fairly quick and efficient method of stripping. It is ideal for keying a painted surface ready for re-painting.
DISADVANTAGES: a harsh method, which removes the surface of the wood as well as the finish. It produces a great deal of dust, so make sure the room is well-ventilated and wear a face mask; if possible perform sanding outside.

1 Start sanding with the random orbital sander fitted with coarse grade abrasive paper. Set the speed to the manufacturers' recommendation for the material you are sanding. Hold the sander firmly against the surface to be sanded but do not exert heavy downwards pressure. Move the sander continuously over the surface; this will minimize the risk of swirl marks.

2 Change the sanding disk as soon as it becomes clogged up with paint. When most of the paint has been removed, switch to a medium grade paper.

3 Use the pointed end of the pointed base to sand into tight corners and the appropriate shaped profile to sand any curved areas or mouldings.

4 Sand thoroughly all over with the finest grade abrasive paper wrapped around a block until the surface is smooth and ready for re-finishing.

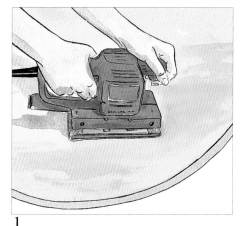

1

2

3

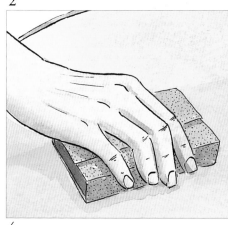

4

STRIPPING WOODEN FLOORBOARDS

If you are lucky enough to have wooden floorboards that are in reasonable condition it is well worth spending time restoring them. However, if you use a floor sander it will create a great deal of dust, so take care to seal the doorway to stop dust escaping into the rest of the house.

STRIPPING WITH WOODEN FLOOR CLEANING SOLUTION
SUITABILITY: only for floorboards with a waxed finish that are in relatively good condition. Then, simply give a good clean before re-finishing.
ADVANTAGES: a gentle method leaving the surface of the wood intact. No hiring costs for sanding equipment.

1

DISADVANTAGES: a time-consuming method. It will not remove paint or varnish finishes.

1 Sweep the floor thoroughly to remove all traces of dust. A cloth dampened in white spirit will remove any final traces of dust.

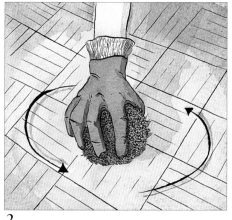

2

2 Apply the floor cleaning solution with medium grade wire wool, working it well into the grain using circular motions. Discard the wire wool as it becomes dirty and clogged up, then carry on with a fresh piece. Work all over the floor surface until the bare wood is exposed.

STRIPPING WITH A HEAVY-DUTY SANDING MACHINE

SUITABILITY: all varieties of solid wooden floorboards and parquet floors.
ADVANTAGES: the quickest and most effective method of stripping back to bare wood. Belt sanders and edging sanders are widely available for hire.
DISADVANTAGES: it removes the top layer of wood leaving the floor looking too new with none of its natural patina. An enormous amount of dust is produced with this method: if possible seal up doorways to other rooms with polythene sheets and open windows for ventilation. It is very noisy: wear ear plugs and warn close neighbours.

1   Prepare floorboards carefully, any nails or screws protruding above the surface of the boards must be driven well below the surface with a nail punch or screwdriver. (If left they will damage the sanding machine.)

2   Start with the belt sander – fitted with a coarse or medium sanding belt – in one corner of the room. Before turning it on, tilt the machine back, switch on and immediately move forwards across the room in a diagonal direction. Never allow the machine to run continuously on one spot, as this will make a deep groove in the floor.

3   When you reach the opposite corner tilt the machine back then turn it off. Turn the machine round and reposition it to move back across the room. Continue this pattern until you have covered the whole room. If there are any traces of the old finish left, repeat the process removing the surface wood until the floorboards are bare.

4   Fit a coarse or medium grade sanding disc to the rotary edging sander and work your way around the edges of the room working as tightly into the corners as possible.

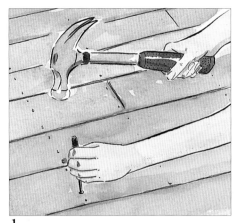

1

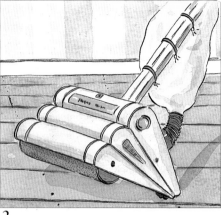

2

3

4

5   Change the medium disc to a fine grade sanding disc on the edging sander. Make your way back around the edges of the room making sure all areas are sanded. (Completing the edges at this stage will prevent you from treading all over the newly stripped floor at a later stage).

Go back to the belt sander and change the belt to a fine grade one. As before, tilt the machine back and then turn it on. Push the machine forwards along the length of the boards following the direction of the grain.

Sweep up, then vacuum the room removing as much dust as possible. To remove dust particles from the air, use water sprayed from a plant misting spray, which will encourage the dust to settle. Finally wipe the entire floor with a cloth soaked in white spirit. Allow to dry thoroughly before re-finishing.

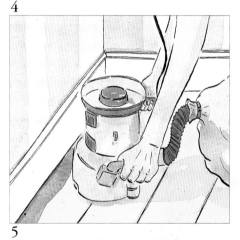

5

Hints and Tips

Once you have stripped the floorboards, it is important to seal them with a finish as soon as possible. Try to avoid walking on the stripped floor with outdoor shoes until it has been sealed because the untreated wood will mark easily.

STRIPPING WITH WHITE SPIRIT

SUITABILITY: removes wax and oil finishes on wood.

ADVANTAGES: it is a gentle but effective stripping method.

DISADVANTAGES: it only works on items that are finished with wax or oil. If any harder finish has been applied to the item, white spirit will not remove it. It also has a drying effect on wood that can leave it looking dull and lifeless. This may be rectified by using a wood restorer, which will replenish the oil content of the wood.

Soak a ball of fine grade wire wool in white spirit and apply it to the item using gentle circular movements. Wipe the area with a clean cloth; if when you remove the cloth it is dirty, continue the process until the cloth remains clean and the item is stripped back to bare wood (see **A**).

STRIPPING WITH METHYLATED SPIRIT

SUITABILITY: removes shellac-based finishes from solid wood.

ADVANTAGES: this is the gentlest method of removing traditional French polish and other shellac-based finishes.

DISADVANTAGES: it does not work with other finishes – veneered items, in particular, as the water content of the spirit raises the grain. It is a fairly messy process because the polish becomes very sticky.

Soak a ball of fine grade wire wool in methylated spirits and apply to the surface – a shellac-based finish will quickly become tacky and will lift off easily with the wire wool. Replace the wool frequently as it soon becomes clogged up with polish. Continue until the wood is bare (see **B**).

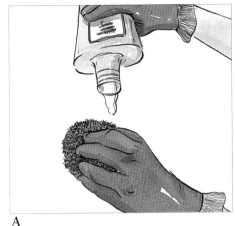

A

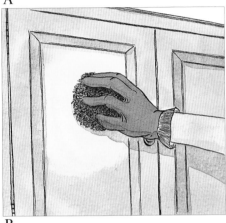

B

Preparing the surface

Once you have stripped the old finish, assess and repair any surface damage – fill holes and dents with filler, obscure any wood knots with knotting solution and re-stick damaged areas with glue. A carefully prepared, super-smooth surface will ensure a good finish.

A

PREPARING FOR A PAINTED OR TRANSLUCENT FINISH

Once a piece of furniture or woodwork is stripped back to bare wood preparing the surface is vital to achieve a professional-looking finish. Having removed the painted or translucent finish it becomes easier to assess the true condition of the item. It also gives you the opportunity to discover the quality of the wood, which helps you determine the type of finish to apply.

WHITE SPIRIT

This is used to neutralize the chemicals in paint and varnish stripper. Apply sparingly with fine grade wire wool or a cloth. As white spirit has a high water content, it will raise the wood grain slightly and will need sanding well afterwards. Do not apply white spirit to fine veneer or marquetry surfaces.

KNOTTING SOLUTION

It is important to use this on any wood with knots in the grain; these are resinous and can spoil subsequent paint finishes with dark stains. Seal knots with several coats of knotting solution before re-finishing (see **A**, on page 24).

PRIMING/SEALING WOOD

It is important to use primer on new or unsealed wood as it prevents the wood from absorbing the subsequent coats of paint. It is possible to buy a combined primer and undercoat specifically designed to provide a hard-wearing base for painting interior woodwork. Make sure you choose the correct oil- or water-based formulation for the top coat you intend to use. Apply with a brush in the direction of the grain, and sand lightly with wet-and-dry paper before applying your chosen finish (see **B**).

WOOD BLEACH

Commercial wood bleach is available, which can be used to reverse the slight darkening effect of some chemical strippers. It can also be used for the removal of dark water marks and rings. Always carry out a test patch on an inconspicuous area and follow manufacturers' instructions (see **C**).

WOOD RESTORER

This is an oil-based liquid, which helps nourish dried-out wood; it is useful if you wish to use a clear, natural-looking oil or wax finish. Wood restorer counteracts the harsh effects of the chemical stripper used on an item. It is easily applied with a cloth and then left to penetrate the wood before a new finish is applied. Before using, check manufacturers' instructions to make sure it is compatible with the finish you wish to apply (see **D**).

REPAIRS WITH GLUE

Any repairs to items, which are to receive a clear finish, should be made before sanding – this will prevent glue getting on the surface of the piece. Most glues will leave a residue, even after wiping away, which will appear as

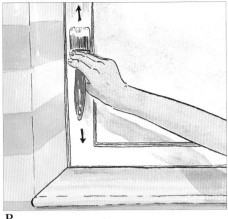

B

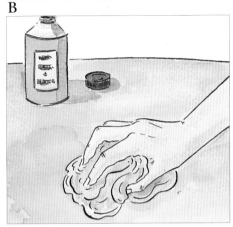

D

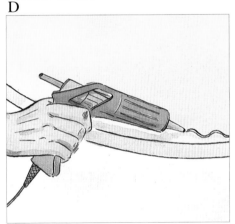

F

a lighter patch beneath a dye or stain when it is applied, or even repel it.

WOOD GLUE/PVA

This white glue, which turns clear when set, is the best glue for sticking wood to wood because it forms a very strong bond that soaks into the fibres of the wood. Useful for most minor repairs, it must be allowed to set overnight. Some awkward repairs can be held in position

C

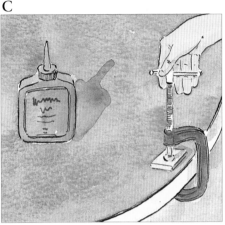

E

Hints and Tips

Take care when using a glue gun to keep your fingers well away from the hot end. Hold small items with a pair of tongs or tweezers because the hot glue will bond instantly to your fingers if touched accidentally causing painful burns. For further protection, wear gloves.

with G-cramps, whereas others will need securing with panel pins or screws while the glue sets (see **E**).

GLUE GUNS

These are useful tools that heat up solid sticks of glue for instant repairs. The glue is applied with a trigger action from the gun and will set in seconds. A variety of glue sticks are available for repairing different items (see **F**).

FILLING

There are numerous types of filler on the market that are formulated to suit different uses. They fill in any holes or cracks making a smooth surface on which to apply the finish

WOOD FILLER

Wood filler, or stopper, is a ready-made paste used for filling wood that is to receive a translucent finish. It is available in a large number of wood shades, but it is also possible to mix colours together until you achieve a shade close to the wood you are filling. It is best applied by pressing it firmly into holes or cracks with a flexible-filling knife then carefully scraping away the excess. For deep or large holes, apply it in layers, allowing each to dry in between coats. Available in water- and oil-based formulations, as well as a variety for outdoor use, it is important to select the appropriate filler for the finish you wish to apply.

A

DECORATORS' FILLER

This is the standard white filler used for mending irregularities in wood and plaster. It is available in powder form, ready-mixed or in a tube. The smooth consistency and quick drying time of this filler make it ideal for use on items that are going to be painted, although it is not suitable for a translucent finish. Apply filler with a flexible filling knife, remove excess with a damp sponge or cloth and leave to dry before sanding (see **A**).

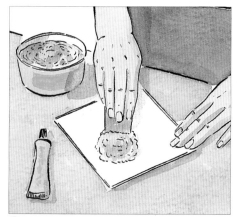

B

TWO-PART CAR BODY FILLER

Although not specifically formulated for use on wood, this filler is excellent for achieving a super-smooth mirror-like finish on most surfaces as it is easily sanded. This makes it suitable for painted and gilded finishes that require a smooth surface. As it is formulated for use on cars, it is also suitable for exterior use. The filler is mixed with a catalyst that starts the hardening process, so only mix the amount you can use within 5 minutes (see **B**).

SANDING

Sanding is essential for creating the ideal surface for a finish as it removes any roughness and smooths the grain. There are many types of abrasive paper available for hand and electric sanding. Electric belt, disc and detail sanders are all useful as they make sanding easier, but for a perfect finish give any item one last sand by hand. Always sand in the direction of the grain, and sand lightly between coats of paint or varnish to remove brushstrokes.

ABRASIVE PAPERS

Abrasive paper is available in many different materials including the common yellow glasspaper, garnet paper, aluminium-oxide paper and wet-and-dry paper. All are available in different grades and the packaging will indicate their uses. When finishing an item, begin with a coarse or medium grade paper, then work your way through the grades finishing with a fine grade. Use extra fine grade abrasive paper or wet-and-dry paper between coats of paint or varnish.

SANDING BLOCKS

These are generally made of cork or rubber, which you wrap the abrasive paper around, however you can use an off cut of wood. For sanding detailed mouldings, flexible sanding blocks are available that have an abrasive surface; these blocks are re-usable and can be cleaned under running water. Alternatively, wrap the appropriate grade of abrasive paper around a shaped block of wood.

SANDING WHEELS

These are special attachments for an electric drill consisting of small pieces of abrasive paper attached around a circular centre piece. When in use, this rotates making it ideal for sanding awkward or rounded surfaces, such as chair backs, legs and spindles (see **A**).

A

ELECTRIC SANDERS

A variety of electric sanders are now available, many of which include several different sanding attachments for different jobs. Some come with built-in dust extraction bags; wood dust is sucked through holes in the abrasive paper, which correspond with holes in the base of the machine. There are even models designed to attach to the hose of a vacuum cleaner.

As there are so many varieties of sander on the market, it is important to choose the one that is most suited to the task. Always use with care and avoid leaving visible scratches by making sure the machine is kept moving.

BELT SANDERS

These are heavy-duty machines with a continuous abrasive belt, which removes a wooden surface very quickly. It is too harsh for use on most furniture apart from large flat pieces such as doors or tabletops (see **B**).

ORBITAL SANDERS

These sanders work by moving a rectangular plate, to which the abrasive paper is clipped, in an orbital motion. Useful for large flat areas (see **C**).

ORBITAL DISC SANDERS

These work in the same way as the orbital, except the plate is circular and made of rubber so it is flexible enough to sand slightly curved surfaces (see **D**).

DETAIL SANDERS

These sanders come in a variety of sizes most of which are rectangular with a pointed end similar in shape to an iron enabling its use in tight corners. They work in an orbital motion (see **E**).

MULTI-SANDERS

These combine the functions of an orbital sander, disc sander and detail sander. Some also have shaped attachments specifically designed for

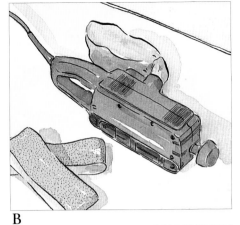

B

C

D

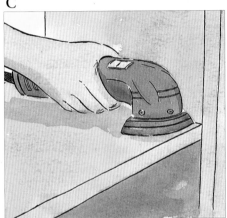

E

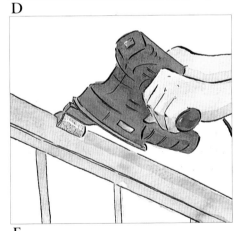

F

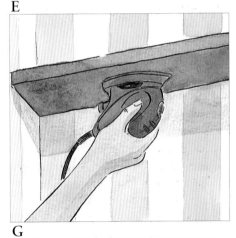

G

sanding different shaped mouldings and beading (see **F**).

PALM SANDERS

These are mini versions of the orbital sander; the main advantage is that they are light weight and easy to use in tight corners or for overhead sanding. They are less powerful than the larger models, but a good option if storage is tight and the item is small (see **G**).

Hints and Tips

If hiring a sanding machine, instructions for fitting abrasive paper should be included. If they are not, ask for a demonstration. Always unplug the machine when changing the paper. Remember to wear a face mask to protect your lungs from wood dust.

PREPARING METAL

As with wood, metal surfaces need to be prepared carefully before receiving a new finish. All ferrous metals, which contain iron and steel, are prone to rust, which forms quickly on unprotected surfaces. Metal that has been previously painted is also highly susceptible to corrosion. This occurs when water seeps through faults in the paintwork eating away at the surface.

WET-AND-DRY PAPER
Before painting any metal item, rub it lightly with a fine grade wet-and-dry paper to roughen the surface giving a key for the paint to adhere to (see **A**).

REMOVING AND PREVENTING RUST
On bare metal, rust convertor/inhibitor should be applied to remove any existing rust and protect it from more forming. Follow manufacturers' instructions, dab it on thickly with an old paintbrush and leave for the recommended length of time before rinsing away the residue (see **B**).

SEALING THE SURFACE
Sealing porous surfaces is important because it reduces the absorption of the finishing coat of paint or varnish, which makes it go further. On hard shiny surfaces, such as metals and plastics it keys the surface giving the paint something to cling to.

SPRAYING WITH PRIMER
On metal that is to be painted, red oxide primer or metal primer should be applied to protect the surface and prevent new rust forming. The easiest way of applying primer to metal is to use a spray formulation; this will cover intricate cast iron mouldings and awkward shapes without leaving visible brush marks. Follow manufacturers' instructions, put down a protective dust sheet and spray the primer evenly

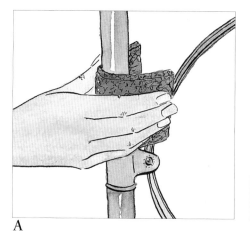

A

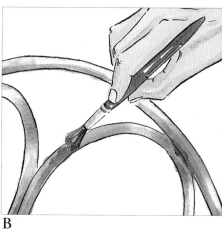

B

C

Hints and Tips

When using spray paints make sure that you are working in a well-ventilated area. It is best to apply several thinly sprayed coats rather than trying to cover with one thick coat that may run. If the paint runs, wait until it is dry, sand the area with wet-and-dry paper then apply another coat.

over the item at a distance of around 35cm (14in). Repeat if necessary until all the metal is covered (see **C**).

REPAIRING DAMAGED METAL
Cast iron items, such as fireplaces are made from molten metal cast in a mould. These items can be brittle and porous, which makes them prone to damage. Cracks and surface defects can be filled with two-part car body filler in the same way as wood items (see page 26). 'Chemical metal', a chemical compound that has the appearance of metal can be used as a filler. Use a two-part epoxy glue for larger jobs.

REPAIRING WITH A SOLDERING IRON
Flat overlapping joints on softer metal items made of copper, brass and tin can be mended using a soft soldering technique. The area to be repaired is first cleaned with a solvent flux. The two areas to be joined are clamped

together with G-cramps. A line of solder is run along the joint and melted into place using an electric soldering iron. The bond formed is much stronger than that made with glue.

REPAIRING SCRATCHED METAL
Metal polish is slightly abrasive and will hide most surface scratches on metal. Rub down deeper scratches using wet-and-dry abrasive paper with a few drops of finishing oil as a lubricant.

CLEAR PROTECTIVE FINISHES
Instead of paint, clear varnish, wax or lacquer can be applied to stripped metal for a protective finish that will not change the surface colour. Copper and brass that is left unfinished, will acquire a patina of verdigris, which can be removed with a rust convertor/inhibitor. Commercial polish will remove tarnishing but a coat of varnish or lacquer will prevent it all together.

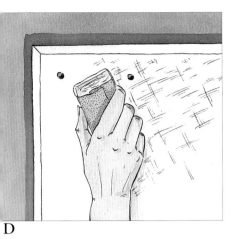

D

SANDING MELAMINE AND OTHER SYNTHETIC SURFACES

Synthetic surfaces are notoriously difficult to paint, as they are shiny and non-porous, which means that there is no surface texture for a new coat of paint to adhere to. To overcome this problem, first key the surface by sanding lightly with wet-and-dry paper or fine grade abrasive paper before priming and painting (see **D**).

Applying the finish

Finishes are applied for many reasons, but mainly to improve the appearance of the piece and to protect the surface against the wear and tear of everyday use. Before applying a finish you should consider carefully whether it will offer adequate protection – for example, a door that will be handled and scuffed regularly will need a tougher finish than a side table used to display decorative items. Also consider the style of the piece – does it lend itself to the intended final finish?

There is a wide range of finishes available. One way of making a choice is to experiment on scrap pieces of timber or metal until you are happy with the results.

TRANSLUCENT FINISHES ON WOOD

As a general rule, hardwoods, such as oak, have a more interesting grain pattern and richer colouring than softwoods like pine, often only requiring a clear protective finish to enhance their appearance. Softwoods tend to be pale in colour and can benefit from a tinted finish, which gives them a richer colour; it also gives the appearance of a more expensive hardwood.

APPLYING VARNISHES

Varnish should be applied with a clean, good quality paintbrush (poor quality brushes are more likely to shed bristles) in a dust-free environment. If possible use a new brush or one reserved for clear finishes to prevent coloured paint streaks or foreign bodies polluting the finish. Load the brush sparingly with varnish (dipping the end of the bristles only), then remove the excess against the lip of the container. Spread the varnish over the surface in different directions, finally finishing with strokes

in the direction of the grain. More than one coat is usually required to give added protection. Follow the manufacturers' advice on drying times and sand lightly between coats with fine grade wet-and-dry paper – this will remove any visible brushstrokes that can occur if you brush over the surface as it is drying (see **A**).

CLEAR VARNISHES

These offer a high degree of protection and are available as either oil- or water-based formulations. Oil-based polyurethane varnishes tend to be yellowish in colour and are the most durable making them suitable for exterior or interior applications. Water-based acrylic varnishes are milky in appearance but dry to a clear finish. You can choose from matt, satin or

A

gloss depending on the degree of 'shine' you require. Clear matt varnish will have an almost invisible effect on the finish, satin varnish will add a subtle sheen, whereas gloss will provide a hard, glossy surface, which will deepen the colour of the grain.

FLOOR VARNISHES

These are specially formulated for sealing and protecting sanded floorboards and usually require several coats for maximum protection.

TINTED VARNISHES

These varnishes are formulated to colour and protect wood. However, unlike woodstain the colours do not penetrate the grain of the wood but sit on the surface making them vulnerable to chipping. They are available in natural wood colours allowing you to deepen and enrich the appearance of pale woods. Tinted varnishes are also available in a wide range of bright and pastel colours, which add transparent colour while allowing the wood grain to show through the finish; they are available in gloss and satin sheen.

WOODSTAINS AND DYES

These liquids are available in a wide choice of colours including natural wood shades. The liquid penetrates the surface of the wood permanently staining it with colour. They are available in both water- and oil-based formulations; the water-based is most widely used as it can be finished with any type of varnish or wax polish. To speed up the process even more, some are available ready mixed with a varnish. Always perform a test patch because different woods have different absorbencies; this will help you work out how many applications of woodstain you will need. If you cannot find the colour you are looking for, it is normally possible to mix woodstains of the same composition together.

APPLYING WOODSTAINS

Care must be taken when using stains. Apply the colour evenly with a paintbrush or pad along the grain of the wood, then wipe over with a soft cloth to remove any excess. It is fairly quick drying which means mistakes are hard to rectify. It is best to build up several thin layers of colour to achieve the desired effect rather than applying too much stain, which will result in runs and drips. Whenever possible apply to the wood in a horizontal position to avoid runs; awkward shapes and vertical surfaces are best stained using a ball of rag. Squeeze out excess stain before applying it (see **A**).

Dab stain onto the end grain of timber with a paintbrush or cloth; this will prevent it becoming darker than the rest of the piece as it is more absorbent than the face of the timber (see **B**).

WOOD WASHES

This is a specific type of colourwash especially designed for use on wood. Emulsion paint is diluted with water to provide a cloudy veil of colour that will allow the grain to show through. This will then need a coat of wax or varnish to seal the surface. The colour is more opaque than a coloured varnish and without shine, which is an advantage if you want a subtle colour. Commercial brands of wood wash are also now available, which are formulated to include a protective matt varnish, although if it is to be used on an item that suffers a lot of wear and tear, most manufacturers recommend additional coats of varnish for protection.

APPLYING WOOD WASHES

Wood wash should be applied with a soft brush or foam applicator in the direction of the wood grain. Apply a thin coat, then build up with additional coats until you are happy with the colour you have achieved (see **C**).

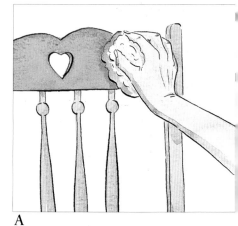

A

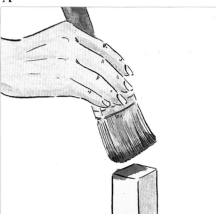

B

Hints and Tips

Liquid wood colours are now available containing wood preservatives that are specially formulated for exterior use. Their main advantage is that they can be applied directly to rough sawn timber, such as fences, without requiring preparation.

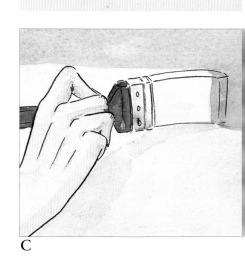

C

Oiled finishes

An oil finish is one of the most natural finishes you can apply as it penetrates and nourishes the wood grain; it is also easy to apply producing a subtle sheen. Oil is a good choice for furniture that may get left outside because it is naturally water-repellent and seals the pores protecting against dirt. It is not a hard finish, which means scratches and knocks show but maintaining the finish is simple as all you need do is wipe over the surface with a little more oil on a cloth. Natural wood kitchen worktops benefit from an application of finishing oil once or twice a year, but check the label to make sure there is nothing toxic in the formulation. Alternatively, olive oil can be used for this purpose. Some hardwoods, such as teak, are naturally oily although they still benefit from the occasional application of oil.

1

DANISH OIL
Danish oil, which is often referred to as finishing oil, is suitable for most interior surfaces because it has a relatively quick drying time.

TEAK OIL
This is the preferred variety of oil for exterior hardwood furniture because it provides a natural water-repellent surface layer on the wood.

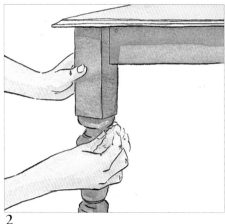

2

APPLYING OIL FINISHES
1 Pour a generous amount of oil onto a clean paintbrush and work it into the wooden surface using small circular movements, which allows the oil to penetrate the wood grain.

2 Remove any excess oil with a cloth and leave to dry (see manufacturers' instructions). Apply up to four layers of oil, then polish with a clean cloth.

Waxed finishes

Wax provides a traditional, soft-looking finish on its own, although it does not offer much protection to bare wood as dirt can easily penetrate it. Wax can be applied over paint or varnish to give it a subtler sheen. A number of different waxes are available including solid, liquid and coloured varieties.

CLEAR WAX
This provides a good neutral finishing polish when applied over another finish; it can also be used to remove excess coloured or liming wax.

LIMING WAX
This is chalky, white coloured wax and is applied with fine grade wire wool to give white highlights to open-grained woods, or to accentuate carvings and mouldings on ornate objects.

1

TINTED WAX
This comes in a variety of colours, which mimic natural wood adding depth and lustre to a finish.

ANTIQUEING WAX
This is a dark blackish colour and is used to give items a patina of age. When applied over a painted surface it will also highlight brushstrokes.

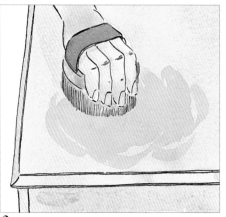

2

APPLYING WAX FINISHES
1 Apply wax to the item using fine grade wire wool in circular movements, which works the wax well into the grain of the wood.

2 Leave the wax to dry, then buff to a brilliant sheen with a soft brush. For a deeper sheen, build up several coats of wax allowing each to dry in between.

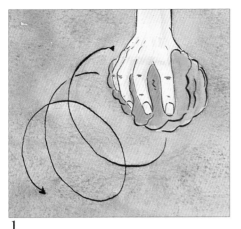

1

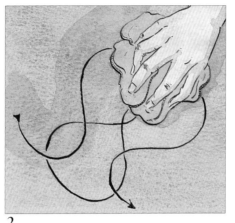

2

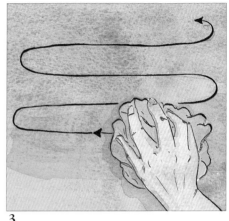

3

FRENCH POLISH/SHELLAC

French polishing is one of the most traditional methods of finishing wooden furniture, and the most difficult to master requiring both patience and elbow grease. When polished, the surface is buffed to a high sheen, but unfortunately this can be easily scratched and marked by heat and water. There are now simpler shellac formulations available, which are simply brushed on. Shellac-based polish is available in a variety of different colours to suit either soft- or hardwoods including white and transparent polish.

APPLYING TRADITIONAL FRENCH POLISH

The traditional method involves applying the polish with a 'rubber' – cotton wool or wadding wrapped up in a linen cloth, which provides an absorbent pad that disperses the polish evenly. Work the pad in circular, then figure of eight movements and finally straight strokes. Add up to 20 coats allowing each one to dry in between. The finished piece does not harden fully for up to a week (see **1**, **2** and **3**).

APPLYING BRUSH-ON FRENCH POLISH

This is a much more straightforward method as the polish is applied with a soft brush. Leave it to dry, then rub down the item with wet-and-dry paper. Add two more coats allowing the polish to dry between each one. Apply a neutral wax polish to the final coat using fine grade wire wool, then buff with a soft cloth to a brilliant sheen.

OPAQUE FINISHES ON WOOD AND METAL

Paint is an ideal finish for wooden items where the surface, colour and grain of the wood are of no interest. It is also a good choice for pieces that will require a lot of filling or repairs that would be obvious through a translucent finish. Many cheaper items of second-hand furniture are utility items from the 1940s and '50s, which are made from cheap plywood and hardboard. Their interest usually lies in their shape, which is best highlighted with a painted finish. There are many different paints available on the market, but as rule oil-based paints are harder wearing and designed for use on wood and metalwork, whereas water-based paints are designed for use on walls and ceilings. Water-based paints can also be used on wood- and metalwork but they will require an additional coat of varnish or wax for protection.

GLOSS PAINT

This is durable, oil-based paint designed specifically for use on wood and metal inside or outdoors. It is traditionally used on interior woodwork including window frames, skirting boards, dado rails, architraves, doors, as well as on copper pipes and radiators. Gloss paint provides a tough, shiny surface and is available in many colours and consistencies including a non-drip variety ideal for painting overhead or vertical surfaces. Gloss paint should be applied thinly over a surface that has been prepared with an oil-based primer.

SATINWOOD PAINT

Satinwood is offered by many paint manufacturers as a mid-sheen alternative to gloss paint and is used in the same situations where a less shiny finish is preferred. Low-odour, acrylic water-based formulation satinwood is becoming more widely available, which many people find more pleasant to use than the oil-based version.

EGGSHELL

This is a traditional trade name for a mid-sheen finish similar to satinwood, which has the same uses. It is available in many historic colour palettes in an oil- or water-based formulation.

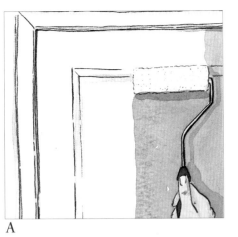

A

APPLYING GLOSS, SATINWOOD AND EGGSHELL PAINTS

These paints should all be applied with a good quality paintbrush or small foam roller over a primed surface. As a rule, the glossier the paint the more obvious the brushstrokes so apply these paints sparingly. Do not overload the brush and spread the paint evenly over the surface. For an extra-fine finish, leave to dry and sand lightly with extra fine wet-and-dry paper before applying a second coat.

Oil-based paints can be thinned down with white spirit and artists' oil paints can be added to tint any of the above oil-based paints. A foam roller is useful for applying these paints to large flat areas, or to radiators, as unwanted brushstrokes can be completely avoided. After use, brushes should be cleaned in white spirit (see **A**).

PAINTING RADIATORS AND HOT WATER PIPES

Before applying paint to radiators and hot water pipes, check manufacturers' instructions as some paints tend to yellow. If in doubt, choose a radiator enamel that is a gloss paint specifically formulated to withstand high temperatures. Turn radiators off and let them cool down before painting.

Special mini rollers (or brushes with long handles) are available for painting behind radiators where a normal paintbrush will not reach (see **B**).

EMULSION PAINTS

These are water-based paints formulated primarily for walls and ceilings; they are available in matt and soft sheen. Some brands also offer kitchen and bathroom emulsion paint, which is more resistant to hot, steamy environments. Emulsion paints can also be used on wood- and metalwork, and are particularly good for creating distressed or rubbed back effects, although they will need a protective top coating of varnish or wax.

APPLYING EMULSION PAINTS

Emulsion paints are easily applied with a paintbrush on small surfaces and with paint pads or rollers on larger surfaces. A primer is not normally required, although a thinned down first coat will provide a smooth surface. Emulsion is very versatile and can be diluted with a little water to create more translucent effects. Clean brushes and rollers with water (see **C**).

SPRAY PAINTS

These paints are applied by aerosol or with a spray gun making them ideal for using on intricate surfaces. They are also a good choice if you want a finish free from brush marks. Spray paints are available in both oil- and water-based formulations – there is a huge variety of colours including metallics. The variety manufactured for cars are good value and ideal for colouring and finishing metal items. There are also special formulations for inhibiting rust and for treating items such as ovens and barbecues that have to withstand high temperatures.

APPLYING SPRAY PAINTS

These are applied by masking the area around the item to be painted. First, shake the aerosol can to mix the contents thoroughly, then spray a thin even coat from a distance of around 25–35cm (10–14in) (see **D**).

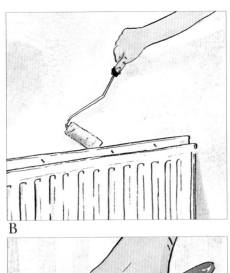

B

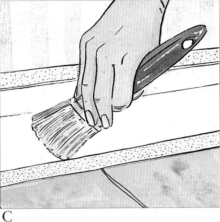

C

LACQUER

This is a type of varnish mainly used in the furniture manufacturing industry. Sprayed onto the finished items, it gives a tough, durable finish. It is also the name given to oriental-style items of lacquerwork, which originated in China. Many coats of lacquer were applied to build up a high sheen. This technique can be replicated today using gloss paint and varnish.

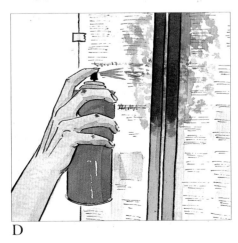

D

Special effects

This term describes any finish that is more elaborate than a simple coat of paint or varnish. Special effects often use clever paint techniques to mimic other materials, or to give the illusion of age.

TWO-COLOUR AGEING

Emulsion can be used to create a number of ageing techniques including two-colour ageing where candle wax is used to create a 'resist', when applied between two coats of emulsion.

1 Apply an even base coat of emulsion paint and leave it to dry. Gently rub candle wax onto the painted surface.

2 Paint the second contrasting colour of emulsion over the waxed surface and leave to dry.

3 Gently rub away the top coat of paint with abrasive paper to expose the base colour beneath the wax concentrating on areas of wear and tear.

4 Seal the surface with a coat of clear wax, applied with fine grade wire wool in gentle circular movements.

CRACKLE GLAZE

This is a decorative finish, which mimics old, peeling paint and can be used on new or old items to give a feeling of age. It works best with two

1

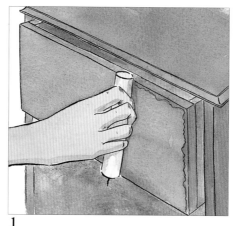

2

3

4

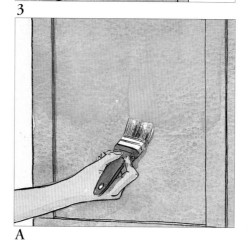

A

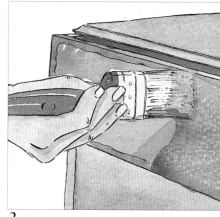

B

strongly contrasting emulsion colours. Having applied the first colour and allowed to dry, the transparent crackle glaze is applied (see **A**).

Paint on the second coat of emulsion. It will react with the glaze causing the paint to 'crack' exposing the first paint colour. It is important to apply this second coat quite thickly being careful not to over-brush the surface (see **B**).

Hints and Tips

Crackle varnish (craquelure) looks particularly effective on small flat areas (it does not work well on curved surfaces) and over decorative effects, such as stencilling or decoupage because it gives the object an instant antiqued appearance.

CRACKLE VARNISH OR CRAQUELURE

This is a water-based technique, which replicates the appearance of old varnish. Often used in conjunction with decoupage, it gives the image an aged appearance. The technique relies on using two coats of varnish, each with a different drying time – the second coat pulls against the first producing a network of hairline cracks.

1 Apply a generous coat of the stage 1 varnish over a previously painted object.

2 Apply the stage 2 varnish in the same way. As it dries, fine cracks will become visible on the surface.

3 With a cloth, apply a little artists' oil or acrylic colour slightly diluted with white spirit (for oil paint) or water (for acrylic paint) rubbing it into the cracks. This emphasizes the crackle effect.

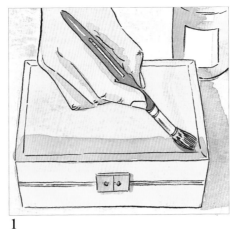
1

2

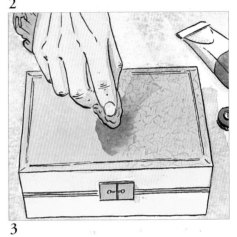
3

GILDING LOOSE AND TRANSFER LEAF

For gilding, thin metal leaf is applied over oil- or water-based size, a type of glue. Traditionally a gesso undercoat was applied to the item before gilding, then sanded to a smooth surface for the metal leaf. Red gesso is the traditional undercoat for gold leaf, yellow for a bright gold finish, and blue or black for silver (see project on page 56).

GILT CREAM

Applied to highlight raised mouldings, carvings and surface details. Gilt cream is the easiest way to apply a gilt sheen, while allowing the base coat of paint to show through. Available in a wide range of colours including metallic shades.

1 Paint the item with several coats of your chosen paint colour bearing in mind that this will show through the gilt cream, and sand down lightly with wet-and-dry paper.

2 Dip your finger tips or a soft cloth in the gilt cream and rub it onto the

surface of the object. Allow to dry before buffing to a sheen with a clean soft cloth.

3 Some makes of gilt cream require a coat of special varnish to fix them permanently – follow manufacturers' instructions.

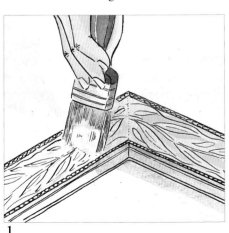
1

2

3

Troubleshooting

Here are some common problems that you may come across before, during or after the stripping and finishing process. Most of these are easy to remedy as there are many products on the market designed to solve specific problems. However, is important to select a product that is compatible with the item and your chosen finish. Always read manufacturers' instructions and wear protective clothing where applicable.

Some damage to the finished surface can be rectified without taking the drastic measure of stripping the item back to the bare material. However more serious problems, such as woodworm, must be treated with care because it can spoil the finish and spread to other items.

WOODWORM

This is actually caused by a beetle, not a worm, and is easy to recognize as the wooden item will be dotted with small holes. It is usually difficult to tell whether the woodworm is still active because the small larvae of the beetle can live within the wood for several years, slowly tunnelling to the surface. New worm holes will look light and there may be a powdery residue of sawdust around them; older holes will be dark in colour and have often been stopped up with polish over the years.

If in doubt, treat with a preparatory woodworm fluid using the applicator provided in the pack, or use an old paintbrush to work the fluid into the holes. If you are stripping the item, lightly brush over it with the woodworm fluid once the wood is bare.

On items that you do not intend to strip, use a furniture polish, which also incorporates an insecticide. Seriously damaged timber should be cut away and replaced with a new section – this may need to be coloured to match the existing wood. Woodworm holes can be filled with wax – special wood-coloured wax crayons are suitable for use under a wax finish. But if you intend applying a different finish, a neutral wood filler can be used (see **A**).

SCRATCHES

Various scratch removers are available, but do select the one that is compatible with the finish you have applied and be sure to follow the manufacturers' instructions. Some surface scratches will respond to polishing with metal polish. Deeper scratches can be filled with wax sticks, or polish painted onto the scratch (see **B**).

DENTS

Shallow dents to wooden surfaces can respond to steam, which causes the grain to swell. Lay a damp cloth over the dent and gently press the area with a domestic iron. Keep the iron moving to avoid scorching the wood. Allow the wood to settle and dry out, then sand and finish (see **C**).

RING MARKS

White ring marks are a common problem on items that have a soft finish such as wax, oil or French polish. They are usually caused by wet glasses or hot mugs left on an unprotected surface. Many of these marks have not penetrated all the way through the polish and will respond to a 'ring removing' polish or metal

A

B

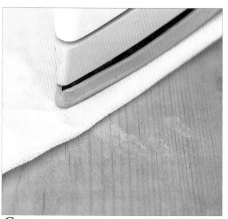

C

polish, which removes the surface coat of polish taking the ring mark with it. The item can then be re-polished. More serious ring marks are darker, they have penetrated through the polish to the bare wood and have soaked into the wood grain. In this case the only solution is to strip the finish around the stain and use a commercial wood bleach on the stain. Wood bleach is applied with an old paintbrush and left to penetrate the wood and lighten the stain. Once neutralized the area can be sanded and re-finished (see **D**).

SCORCH MARKS

These are usually the accidental result of using a hot-air gun to strip the paint. If the hot blistered paint is not scraped away quickly enough from the surface it can scorch the wood beneath leaving a dark burn mark. The only way of removing these marks is to remove the scorched wood using varying grades of abrasive paper, finishing with a fine grade paper to smooth the surface (see **E**).

PLYWOOD

This is a man-made board constructed like a sandwich with thin sheets of wood glued together. There are various different types available; some are faced with attractive hardwoods for furniture making. Cheaper varieties are commonly used in the manufacture of furniture carcasses. It is always worth stripping a test patch on a piece of furniture, as you may find it is constructed from cheap plywood. It is not really worth stripping the item back to the bare plywood because it will not be suitable for a transparent finish. To prepare a plywood item for re-finishing, a thorough sanding will provide an adequate surface for painting over. However, if the piece is a mixture of plywood and another wood, you may wish to strip it back and apply different finishes to each section.

WOOD KNOTS

These are recognizable as dark rings on planed timber. They are the areas where small branches grew from the main trunk of the tree and need to be treated before the wood is finished. Loose knots are a sign of poor quality timber and, if the knot has fallen out leaving a hole, it will need to be filled with wood filler (stopper) before finishing. Most knots are resinous meaning sap continues to seep from the knot even after finishing. This can cause 'bleeding' through the paintwork and dark yellow sap will appear on the surface of the wood. There is no need to treat knots if you are applying a clear finish because this will be enough to seal them. However, if you are going to apply a painted finish, it is essential to paint on the knots a knotting solution that is made of shellac, which will stop resin seeping through the paintwork (see **F**).

RUST

Before giving bare metal a new finish, it is essential to remove any rusty areas and treat them with rust convertor/inhibitor to prevent the rust returning. Patches of flaky rust can be removed with a wire brush or a rust removing scourer. Rust will form on any ferrous metals that contain iron or steel, so if they are to be painted they should be primed first with a rust-inhibiting primer, then painted with an oil-based paint. If you have an item that is going to receive a clear finish, or iron polish/paste, treat it with a rust convertor/inhibitor, which you paint on and leave to penetrate the surface. When treating cast iron, remember that the surface can be scratched quite easily so take care with scraping tools. Use the finest grade wire wool when applying finishing products.

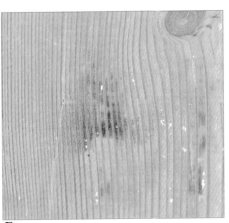

D

E

F

Cast iron fireplace with graphite finish

Due to ever-changing fashions, period pieces such as this ornate fireplace are subjected to inappropriate decorating experiments. It is generally much better to restore the piece and pair it with complementary decor.

Planning your time

DAY ONE

AM: Loosen rust with scourer. Apply paint stripper, then laminated paper

PM: Remove paper to strip off paint. Apply rust convertor, then clean off

DAY TWO

AM: Cover with iron paste. Buff up with cotton cloth

PM: Paint shelf, then treat with iron paste. Fix shelf to fireplace

Tools and materials

Heavy-duty rubber gloves

Scourer

Blanket paint stripper with laminated paper kit

Plastic spreader

Scrubbing brush

Rust convertor/inhibitor

Fine grade wire wool

Iron paste/polish

Old paintbrush

Cotton cloths

Shop-bought pine shelf with smooth, rounded edge

Black emulsion paint

Paintbrush

Many cast iron fireplaces are painted white because they are considered too dark and ornately fussy for contemporary interiors. Rather than adapting their decor to balance the heavy appearance of the cast iron, people find it easier to blank them out with a heavy layer of paint. This is a real shame, as a beautifully restored, working fireplace provides a living focal point to a room. As most Victorian and Edwardian homes have at least one remaining fireplace, it is worth spending some time turning it back into a feature, particularly if it is a working fireplace.

If you are thinking of adding a fireplace to a bare chimney breast, hunt around a few architectural salvage yards to see if you can find one of the same period as your house. It is also important to consider the scale of the room and the size of the chimney breast. In general, reception rooms had large fireplaces with separate surrounds, whereas bedroom fireplaces (called 'Registers') were more modest affairs, moulded in one piece of cast iron.

When stripped of layers of paint and sealed with iron paste, cast iron takes on the look of silvery graphite, which catches the light beautifully. Despite its hardness, cast iron is actually a porous material and is easily scratched, so any stripper applied to the surface must be neutralized with water once it is removed. In this case, a blanket stripping method, using a kit including stripping paste and a special laminated paper ('blanket') was the best option. Once all the paint is removed it is a wise precaution to treat the fireplace with rust convertor, which also acts as an inhibitor. Then the polish is simply applied with a brush or cloth and buffed to a brilliant sheen.

For this project, the fireplace was missing its mantle shelf. This was easily replaced by a ready-made shelf, painted black and treated with iron paste. Once polished, the shelf took on the same graphite sheen as the cast iron and was fitted in place on the wall with mirror plates.

1

2

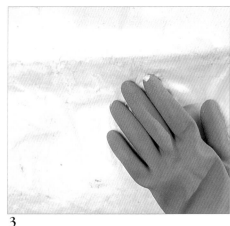

3

Day One

Step 1

Wearing heavy-duty gloves, use a rust-removing scourer to loosen and remove any flaky surface rust before applying stripper.

Step 2

Using the spreader, dab a thick layer of blanket stripper all over the surface of the fireplace. Take particular care to push the paste into any moulded areas to ensure a consistent paste thickness.

Step 3

Once the fireplace is completely covered with stripper, carefully smooth the laminated paper cover over it, working from the centre outwards pressing it into the paste. Leave for the manufacturers' recommended waiting time – this is determined by the thickness of the paint to be removed.

Step 4

Check on the stripping action of the paste at regular intervals. When you are satisfied that it has loosened as much paint as possible, carefully lift the hardened paint, paper and stripper, and dispose carefully.

Step 5

Use plenty of clean water and a stiff scrubbing brush to remove any remnants of paint and to neutralize the surface of the cast iron.

4

5

Hints and Tips

It is easiest to strip large items, such as fireplaces, outdoors, laid flat on the ground. This will not be possible with fitted fireplaces, so take care to protect the surrounding floor and wall areas with plastic sheeting and plenty of newspaper. Remember to neutralize the surface with water.

6

7

Step 6
Apply rust convertor/inhibitor to any remaining areas of rust and leave to penetrate the surface for at least half an hour, before carefully removing with fine grade wire wool.

Day Two

Step 7
Once the surface of the fireplace is completely dry and free from paint and rust, apply a thin layer of iron paste using an old paintbrush, or cloth, and allow to dry for at least half an hour.

Step 8
Rub the fireplace with a clean soft cloth until it shines with a graphite finish.

Step 9
Take the shop-bought pine shelf (of the same length and depth as the fireplace) and apply several thick coats of black emulsion paint. Leave to dry.

Step 10
Cover the shelf with a thin layer of iron paste (still wearing your gloves). Once dry, buff the shelf to a brilliant sheen.

Fix the shelf to the fireplace – if you are not sure how to do this, it is best to seek professional advice.

8

9

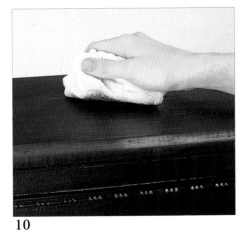

10

Garden bench with crackle glaze paint

A distressed paint finish in two muted shades was the perfect way to finish this old garden bench. The soft colours complement the surrounding foliage providing a tranquil spot to sit and admire the garden.

Planning your time

DAY ONE

AM: Scrape off paint and apply wood hardener to rotten areas

PM: Apply rust convertor. Sand thoroughly

DAY TWO

AM: Apply base coat. Paint on crackle glaze and leave to dry

PM: Paint on top coat. Apply several coats of varnish

Tools and materials

Wire brush

Wood filler

Plastic scraper

Wood hardener

Old paintbrush

Coarse grade abrasive paper

Electric sander or sanding block, fitted with fine grade abrasive paper

Drill and wire brush drill attachment

Rust convertor/inhibitor

Fine grade wire wool

Fine and medium paintbrushes

Lubricant

Two shades of water-based paint

Crackle glaze

Exterior oil-based varnish

Good quality, hardwood garden furniture will last for years if properly maintained with an annual coat of teak or linseed oil to nourish the wood. However furniture that has been neglected or left unfinished gradually looses its water-repellent coating, which allows damp to penetrate and mould to grow. This furniture is also likely to dry out and crack in the summer months leaving it damaged and unattractive.

Even these neglected pieces are not beyond rescue, although it is best to work with the 'distressed look' rather than against it. If the piece has been left outside for some time, remaining paint can often be scraped off with a paint scraper. But if it is damp and mouldy, it is important to eliminate these problems before attempting to re-finish the piece – there are a number of wood hardening products available that stop rot in its tracks. It is also best to leave the piece indoors or in a garage to allow it to dry out thoroughly before re-finishing.

This bench was given a coat of crackle glaze between two contrasting colours of water-based paint. The top coat of paint reacts immediately with the crackle glaze, so that the cracks appear as the glaze is applied, but do not 'over-brush' because this will interrupt the chemical process. Each brand of crackle glaze will have a slightly different drying time, so always follow the manufacturers' instructions.

Applying a simple, distressed finish where a base coat of paint will show through the top coat gives the illusion of age, which works well against garden foliage. However to protect the finish, it is vital to apply several coats of an exterior grade polyurethane varnish, which can be reapplied every couple of years as necessary.

Wood-washed door with etched glass panels

Most older houses have internal doors that could be improved with a new finish. Updating a Victorian door with wood wash allows the wood grain to show through, as well as removing the yellowness of stripped pine.

Planning your time

DAY ONE

AM: Use hot-air gun and scrapers to remove paint

PM: Fill cracks and holes. Sand down and clean door

DAY TWO

AM: Apply two coats of wood wash. Adhere star stickers to glass panels

PM: Spray glass with etching spray. Varnish door and replace fittings

Tools and materials

Screwdriver

Hot-air gun and heat deflector attachment

Goggles

Shaped paint scraper

Fine grade wire wool

Liquid paint stripper

Heavy-duty rubber gloves

Cabinet scraper

Neutral wood filler and filling knife

Electric sander or block fitted with fine grade abrasive paper

Tack rag

White spirit

White wood wash or diluted emulsion paint

Paintbrush or foam applicator

Paper and adhesive tape

Self-adhesive stars

Glass etching spray

Tweezers

Matt acrylic varnish

Door furniture of choice

This Victorian, half-glazed door was unearthed at a local architectural salvage yard. With a small amount of trimming it was made to fit the doorway between a dining room and kitchen, replacing the plywood door that hung there. Most salvage yards stock unstripped doors of various sizes; they then send the door away to be acid dipped. Although this is a quick stripping method, it weakens the joints and can dissolve all the glue; items also return with a dry, bleached appearance as many of the natural oils have been stripped away. This door came with its original paint finish intact, so it was possible to use a gentler stripping technique.

Doors are good projects for beginners as they have so many flat planes, which makes stripping easier. As this door was heavily painted with gloss paint, a hot-air gun was used to strip it. This method is particularly suited to gloss paint as it is a fairly brittle finish that comes off quite cleanly when heat is applied.

The time-consuming part of stripping a door is removing the paint from the corners of the panels and from the glazing beads. Once the clean pine beneath was exposed, it became evident that this door was covered in dents, cracks and filled holes that would be clearly visible under a completely translucent finish such as varnish or wax. Applying a wood wash was a good compromise, while letting the pattern of the grain show through, it made past repairs to the door blend in and appear less noticeable. The subtle veil of white wood wash also toned down the yellowness of the newly stripped pine.

An etching spray was used to add a decorative finish to the clear glass; this is semi-permanent and can be removed with a scraper if mistakes are made or a new pattern is required. To complete the face-lift, a crystal door knob and chrome escutcheon (both purchased from the same salvage yard) were fitted.

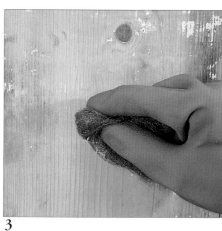

1

4

5

Day One

Step 1

Remove existing door furniture. Wearing goggles, direct a hot-air gun at the surface, wait for the paint to bubble up and blister, then scrape off with the paint scraper.

Step 2

Fit the heat deflector attachment. Hold the heat gun next to the glazing beads with the solid metal side of the shield between the heat gun and the glass panels. With the other hand, remove paint with the scraper.

Step 3

To remove any paint residue, pour liquid paint stripper onto a ball of fine grade wire wool and scrub with a circular motion. Remember to wear protective gloves.

Step 4

Strip stubborn paint from corners of panels and glazing beads with a cabinet scraper. Hold at an angle of 70°, pull down firmly and the brittle paint should shatter.

Step 5

With a filling knife, apply neutral-coloured wood filler to any unwanted cracks or holes. Smooth off and allow to dry.

Step 6

Sand down the door (electrically or manually). Remove sawdust with a tack rag moistened with a little white spirit.

6

7

8

9

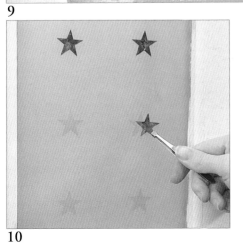

10

11

Day Two

Step 7

Moving in the direction of the grain, apply wood wash in smooth strokes with a paintbrush or foam applicator completing the door panels first, followed by the surrounding areas. Leave to dry, then apply a second coat.

Step 8

Mask off the door with paper and adhesive tape. Clean the glass thoroughly. Apply small adhesive star stickers at measured intervals onto the glass panels.

Step 9

Shake the can of glass etching spray, then spray evenly over the glass panels from a distance of around 10cm (4in). Leave to dry and repeat if necessary.

Step 10

Use a pair of tweezers to remove each sticker carefully.

Step 11

Using a clean paintbrush, apply a layer of matt acrylic varnish to the wood areas of the door. Leave to dry. Apply a second coat of varnish.

Fit the new door furniture in place through the existing holes and screw firmly into place.

Contemporary limed washstand

With a little lateral thinking, this uninspiring side table can be transformed into a beautiful and useful washstand. The limed finish picks out the natural hardwood grain, while the finishing oil makes the surface watertight.

Planning your time

DAY ONE

AM: Strip the table, brush down and apply liming wax

PM: Remove excess lime with finishing oil. Apply neutral wax

DAY TWO

AM: Remove hardboard top

PM: Fit new top and leave to dry. Attach towel rail and plumb in taps

Tools and materials

Heavy-duty rubber gloves

Chemical paint stripper

Fine grade wire wool

Cotton cloths

White spirit

Bronze brush

Liming wax

Finishing oil

Neutral wax polish

Flat scraper

Contact adhesive

Aluminium laminate (cut to size)

Heavy weights (books or bricks)

Bradawl

Drill and hole cutting attachment

Chrome towel rail with rust-resistant chrome screws

Mixer taps

Free-standing washbasin

Small side tables can be easily adapted to make unusual bathroom or bedroom tables. This table with a hardboard top was once a school desk and had been roughly spray painted blue over a previously varnished surface.

A test patch revealed that the table was oak – this is a porous wood particularly suited to a limed finish, which would highlight the grain pattern. To achieve a good limed finish, strip back to bare wood before applying the liming wax.

A limed finish was traditionally achieved using real quicklime, which would deter woodworm and other parasites. Today a user-friendly, non-toxic wax is a safer way to produce the same effect.

The liming process is relatively easy and can be used on a variety of woods with different effects. With porous hardwoods such as oak, a bronze brush is used to 'raise the grain' and the liming paste is absorbed into the pores of the wood. In less grainy softwoods such as pine, the grain cannot be raised so there is no need to brush it; the effect will depend on the pale wax sitting in carved surfaces and mouldings. Large areas such as floorboards also look good with a limed finish.

The hardboard tabletop was replaced with an aluminium laminate, which provides a wipeable surface for the table. Then, with the help of a professional plumber, mixer taps were plumbed in, a free-standing washbasin positioned underneath and the table was converted to a guest bedroom washstand.

Day One

Step 1

Wearing heavy-duty rubber gloves, strip the table using the chemical paint stripper and fine grade wire wool until all remnants of paint and varnish have been removed.

Neutralize the paint stripper by wiping the piece down with a cloth dampened with white spirit. Allow to dry.

Step 2

Brush the table vigorously with the bronze brush in the opposite direction to the grain – you should be able to see the grain rise and the surface will feel slightly rough.

Step 3

Dip a large piece of wire wool in the liming wax and rub it all over the table legs and frame, working it well into the grain. It will look very white at this stage. Leave the wax to dry for approximately 5 minutes.

Step 4

Take a clean cloth dampened with finishing oil and apply it to the table removing excess liming wax. Allow to dry, then apply several coats of neutral wax polish. When dry, buff to a sheen with a soft cloth.

1

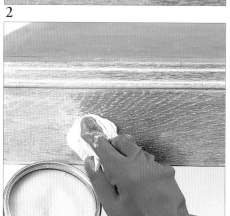

2

3

4

Hints and Tips

To achieve a waterproof finish, remove excess liming wax with a finishing oil. If this is not required, just use neutral wax. To maintain the finish, simply add additional coats of neutral wax. When liming softwoods that do not have a coarse grain, there is no need for a bronze brush.

5

Day Two

Step 5
Remove the vinyl surface of the table, carefully scraping the whole area until it is completely flat.

Step 6
Spread contact adhesive over the tabletop and the underside of the aluminium laminate and allow to go tacky (this will take approximately 10–15 minutes).

Step 7
Carefully place the laminate into position on the tabletop and weigh down with heavy books or bricks. Allow to dry for several hours (following manufacturers' instructions) before removing the weights.

Step 8
To fit the towel rail use a bradawl to make guide holes for the screws, then screw into place using rust-resistant chrome screws.

If you wish to make the table into a washbasin support, measure the diameter of the basin wastepipe and cut a hole the corresponding size in the tabletop using a hole cutting drill attachment. Repeat the process for the taps. Unless you are proficient, a plumber will be needed to plumb the basin and taps into a nearby water supply.

6

7

8

Gilded mirror frame with antiqued varnish

A restored, ornate mirror is ideal for adding a touch of bygone opulence to a room. With a little work, it is possible to repair intricate moulding and the application of metal leaf and shellac provide that distressed look.

Ornate mirrors are popular collector's pieces as they add interest and drama to a room. A well-placed mirror creates a focal point and gives the illusion of increased light and space. Traditionally mirrors were hung above fireplaces but they look equally good propped on a shelf or leaning against a wall in any position where you would like extra light or sparkle.

It is still possible to pick up ornate mirrors for a reasonable price if you are willing to invest a bit of time and effort in the repair. Often delicate mouldings have been broken off and fragile 'silvered' glass has become scratched and mottled. Signs of age give mirrors of this type character, so it is important when restoring them not to go overboard. Although the finest examples were hand carved from wood, many detailed mouldings were added to the basic wooden frame, which were made of moulded plaster or resin fixed over a wire armature.

If your mirror has a gilt finish that is too damaged to live with, first remove the flaky finish with the gentle use of a stiff brush. To take the finish back to wood and plaster, a liquid paint stripper is ideal because it can be rubbed into detailed mouldings with the aid of a nylon-bristled toothbrush.

When the frame is stripped, carefully smooth it with wire wool to a super-smooth finish that is ideal to gild over. Most gilded items are first painted with gesso (an undercoat and sealer that can also be used to fill the grain of unpainted wood), which looks attractive when visible through a distressed finish. Traditionally a rich red was used under gold, and dark blue or black under silver. However, you can buy white gesso and paint it in a colour of your choice to complement the large choice of metal leaf finishes available. Metal leaf comes in a choice of transfer, which is supplied on wax-backed paper, or loose form. For frames with intricate mouldings, loose leaf is the most effective form as it can be easily pushed into moulded and difficult-to-reach areas.

Planning your time

DAY ONE

AM: Apply stripper then remove with white spirit to neutralize

PM: Make repairs with self-hardening clay putty

DAY TWO

AM: Paint with gesso. Apply gold size, leave until tacky

PM: Cover with metal leaf then rub away in areas. Apply varnish. Finish with a coat of amber shellac

Tools and materials

Heavy-duty rubber gloves

Paint and varnish stripper

Old paintbrush

Fine and coarse grade wire wool

Nylon-bristled toothbrush

White spirit

Two rolls of self-hardening clay putty

Clay-modelling tools

Gesso

Fine paintbrushes

Gold size

Talcum powder

Transfer or loose metal leaf

Soft cloth or soft-bristle brush

Sharp scissors

Clear varnish

Amber shellac varnish

Day One

Step 1

Wearing heavy-duty rubber gloves, apply the stripper with an old paintbrush. Leave for around 10 minutes; remove a test patch to see if the painted finish comes away easily.

Step 2

Remove loosened paint with fine grade wire wool. Use a nylon-bristled toothbrush to force more stripper into the carved mouldings and details. Continue until all the finish is removed.

Step 3

Rub the frame down with coarse grade wire wool dipped in white spirit to neutralize it, so that the surface is smooth and ready for gilding.

Step 4

Knead together equal amounts of the two rolls of self-hardening clay putty until the colours are completely and evenly merged.

Step 5

Use clay-modelling tools to shape replacement leaves and other details onto the frame, and press firmly in place. The putty will also bond any areas of loose moulding to the body of the frame. Leave to dry overnight.

1

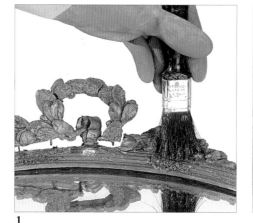

2

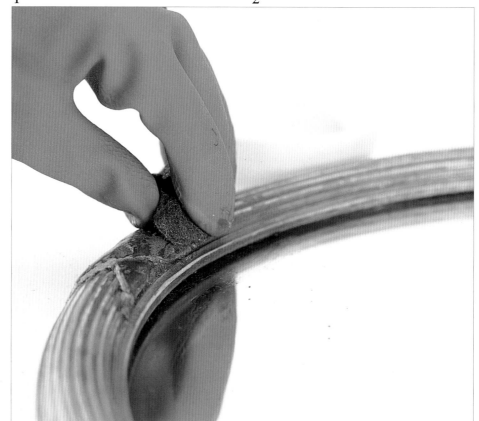

3

4

5

6

7

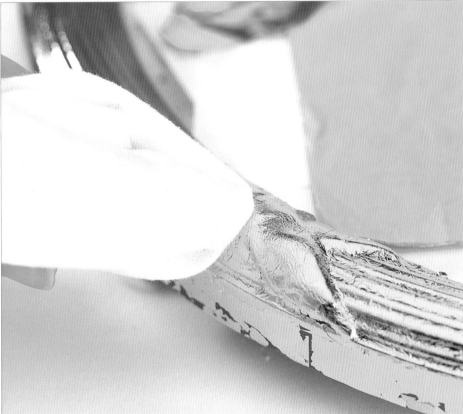

8

9

10

Day Two

Step 6

Paint the entire frame with a layer of gesso and allow to dry. Rub down with fine grade wire wool and repeat for a super-smooth finish. Then apply gold size with another paintbrush and leave until tacky.

Step 7

Dust your fingers with talcum powder to remove the oils. Pick up a sheet of metal leaf and press it down gently onto the gold-sized frame.

Step 8

Use a soft cloth, or soft bristled-brush, to smooth the leaf into place and cut off any excess with a sharp pair of scissors. Continue until the whole frame is covered. Use fine grade wire wool to rub the leaf gently exposing the coloured gesso beneath in certain areas.

Step 9

Apply a thin layer of clear varnish to the whole frame using a clean paintbrush. Leave to dry.

Step 10

For a darker antiqued finish, apply a coat of amber shellac, concentrating on the moulded areas. To achieve an even darker finish, apply another coat.

1950's kitchen cabinet with pearlized paint

Fitting a new kitchen can be a costly affair, so it is worth making an effort to restore existing units or junk shop finds. A well-used cabinet such as this can be successfully mended and given a contemporary finish.

Units like these are fairly easy to come by, although the 'unfitted' look for kitchens is coming increasingly back in vogue. The shape of this piece is typically 1950's, with squared-off corners and door edges that look great with the current retro-style kitchen appliances.

This cabinet would have been used for food storage – one compartment contains small drawers for flour, rice, sugar and other food staples. However, updated with pearlized paint and new door furniture it is smart enough for storing and displaying colourful china and glassware in the dining room.

As this piece is made from a softwood frame with plywood doors it was not worth stripping right back to bare wood. However to achieve a super-smooth paint finish it was essential to sand the whole piece thoroughly. The cabinet was then painted with a low-sheen eggshell paint, which is very hard-wearing. To make the doors contrast with the rest of the unit, they were sprayed with silver paint, which acted as an undercoat for the pearlized paint finish. As the piece was in such a bad state of repair, all the handles and hinges were replaced with new matt silver ones. The glass from the top cabinet doors was missing so they were re-glazed with bevelled glass, in keeping with the 1950's style.

Planning your time

DAY ONE

AM: Remove door furniture and repair broken beading

PM: Sand down then neutralize cabinet. Apply eggshell paint

DAY TWO

AM: Spray doors with silver paint, when dry apply pearlized paint

PM: Make repairs to glazing beads. Replace glass and door furniture

Tools and materials

Screwdriver

Sugar soap

Cotton cloths

PVA glue

Panel pins

Hammer

Nail punch

Wood filler and filling knife

Electric sander and detail sanding attachment

White spirit

Various grades of abrasive paper

Eggshell paint and paintbrush

Fine grade wet-and-dry paper

Sanding block

Silver spray paint

Pearlized two-stage paint finish

Painting pad

Chisel

Fine-nosed pliers

Glass (cut to size)

Electric drill

Door furniture of choice

Day One

Step 1

Remove all the doors, handles and hinges from the cabinet and wipe away dirt and grime with a cloth dipped in soapy water.

Mend the broken beading by re-sticking each piece with a thin layer of wood glue.

Step 2

Fix the beading firmly into position using panel pins and a hammer, then tap the pins below the surface of the wood using a nail punch.

Step 3

Fill the handle and hinge holes, and any damaged areas with wood filler using a filling knife. Leave to dry.

Step 4

Using an electric sander, or sanding block and abrasive paper, give the entire piece a thorough sanding. As the unit is made from a mixture of softwood and plywood, do not attempt to remove all the paint or more filling will be needed to create a completely smooth surface.

1

2

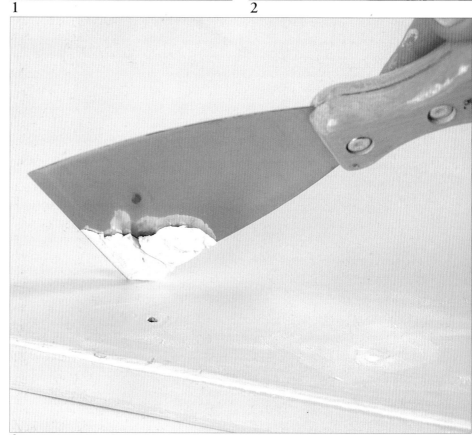

3

4

Hints and Tips

Old screws can be difficult to remove, particularly if the screw head is damaged. If the screw will not turn it may be necessary to saw off the head using a junior hacksaw, then remove the shaft using a claw hammer or a pair of pliers. Fill the resulting hole and leave to dry.

5

Step 5

Use the detail sanding attachment to make sure awkward areas such as the shelf fronts are properly sanded. Remove all dust from the cabinet using a cloth moistened with white spirit. Leave to dry.

Step 6

Coat the entire cabinet with a layer of eggshell paint and leave to dry. Sand with fine grade wet-and-dry paper before applying a second coat.

Day Two

Step 7

Spray the cabinet doors with two coats of silver paint sanding with fine grade wet-and-dry paper in between each coat.

Step 8

Apply the pearlized paint finish in long, smooth strokes to each door using a painting pad to avoid brush marks. Leave to dry.

6

7

8

9

Step 9

Rub over the dry pearlized paint with wet-and-dry paper wrapped around a sanding block. Apply another coat of paint.

Step 10

Remove existing glazing beads (wood that secures glass to the door) using the end of a chisel to prize them off carefully.

Step 11

Use a pair of fine-nosed pliers to remove any protruding panel pins.

10

11

12

Step 12
Place the sheet of new glass in the recess and tap the glazing beads back into position securing with panel pins. Repeat for the other door.

Step 13
Mark and drill small pilot holes for the new cabinet handles and hinges. Fix them securely into position.

13

Hints and Tips

When hanging cabinet doors, it is much easier to lie the cabinet on its back, if possible: this prevents gravity working against you. It is also advisable to ask a friend to hold the door in place while you mark out hinge positions. Hinges can be adjusted by tightening and loosening the screws.

Oak ladder back chair with natural oil finish

Inherited or reclaimed wooden furniture is often too dark and heavy-looking for contemporary homes. But this problem can be easily overcome by stripping the wood to its original state and applying a lighter finish.

O ak is a hardwood with a distinctive open grain pattern. It is a favourite with traditional furniture makers, who often finish it with a dark wax or stain. This rustic, ladder back chair is part of an inherited set, which has a pleasing shape but the dark finish was too heavy for a contemporary interior. On close inspection it was obvious that several different finishes had been applied to the chair, including wax polish, varnish and shellac-based polish. For this reason a chemical paint and varnish stripper was used to remove them all. The absorbent nature of the wood combined with years of polish, as well as the complicated shape of the chair make it quite a tricky item to

strip, so allow one whole day for the stripping alone. The final finish is quick to apply and simple to maintain.

Having carefully stripped away the old dark finish to reveal the attractive grain and natural colour of the oak, use a traditional finish that will let the beauty of the wood shine through. Stripping revealed that some areas of the chair were darker than others, so a medium oak woodstain was applied to achieve a consistent colour. The harsh stripping chemicals can remove a lot of the natural oils in wood, but a wood restorer will replenish them. The chair was finished with one of the most natural finishes available, Danish oil. An oiled finish is not particularly hard-wearing but it gives the piece an attractive, natural-looking sheen, which can be built up with additional applications – this will nourish the wood and keep it looking its best.

Day One

Step 1

Wearing gloves, brush stripper on the chair. Leave it for a few minutes to penetrate the finish before carefully removing with fine grade wire wool. Repeat over the entire surface of the chair until the majority of the finish is removed. As the wire wool becomes clogged up, replace with a fresh piece.

Step 2

Sand the chair using the fine grade abrasive paper wrapped around the sanding block – paying particular attention to stubborn areas – until all the dark patches disappear from the pores of the wood.

Step 3

On curved areas, such as the turned spindles, use a sanding wheel fitted to an electric drill to access hard-to-reach areas. Replace the abrasive paper regularly as it becomes clogged up, moving to finer grade paper to finish the surface. Alternatively, cut sheets of medium grade abrasive paper into lengths and wrap it around the spindle holding the ends with each hand. Gently pull with alternate hands until the clean surface is revealed.

Step 4

Give the chair a final sanding with fine abrasive paper to smooth the surface ready for re-finishing. Use a tack rag moistened with a little white spirit to remove any remaining sawdust and neutralize any remnants of chemical stripper.

1

2

3

Hints and Tips

Due to its porous nature, oak stains easily and even stripped wood can retain dark marks. These can be removed with additional sanding, or in extreme cases with wood bleach although this will lighten the wood. To return the wood to its natural shade, apply a commercial woodstain.

4

5

7

6

Day Two

Step 5

Apply the medium oak woodstain with a foam applicator all over the chair using long strokes in the direction of the grain. Use a cloth to remove any excess and allow to dry. Add a second coat of woodstain to areas that appear lighter, which will even out the colour.

Step 6

Using a soft cloth, apply wood restorer to the chair rubbing in circular movements to ensure it penetrates the grain. Leave to dry.

Step 7

With a clean cloth, apply Danish oil using small circular movements. Leave to dry, then repeat several times. Once the oil has had time to penetrate the wood, and is no longer oily to the touch, polish to a brilliant sheen with a dry cloth.

Bedside table with silver leaf finish

The bedside table is an invaluable piece of furniture for housing an infinite assortment of bedtime clutter. Even this utility piece can be given an all-over treatment to mask its poor points and highlight its design features.

This pretty bedside table was an ideal candidate for restoration because of its elegant form and detailed claw feet. Despite its pleasing shape, it is probably a piece of utility furniture (so called because it was made fairly cheaply after the Second World War). Good quality wood was scarce at that time, so it was used only for the legs and frame, while the top and shelf were made from cheaper plywood.

Having stripped the piece back to bare wood it was apparent that the top needed a lot of repair work and a replacement drawer, so it was simplest to paint the table and then apply a solid painted finish followed by silver transfer leaf, which is actually made from thin sheets of aluminium. If silver is not to your taste, replace it with gold or copper leaf. It is easy to change the appearance of the finish by experimenting with different colours underneath. Blue and black are traditionally applied under silver, whereas red and yellow sets off gold to best effect.

To give the piece a patina of age, the silver leaf finish was distressed using wire wool to expose the deep blue base colour. The finish was then protected with several coats of matt varnish. The missing drawer was replaced with a false drawer front made from a single panel of wood glued into place; moulded panels were also added to echo the bowed front of the piece.

Planning your time

DAY ONE

AM: Strip existing paint finish. Fill cracks and holes with wood filler

PM: Glue and cramp warped plywood tabletop

DAY TWO

AM: Sand then paint table blue. Cut and fit replacement drawer

PM: Gild with metal leaf. Rub areas with wire wool, then varnish

Tools and materials

Heavy-duty rubber gloves

Paint and varnish stripper

Various paintbrushes

Flat paint scraper

Shaped paint scraper

Nylon-bristled toothbrush

Fine grade wire wool

Neutral-coloured wood filler

PVA glue

Wood off cuts

G-cramps

Electric sander (optional)

Fine grade abrasive paper

Sanding block

Blue emulsion

Wet-and-dry paper (optional)

Tape measure

Piece of scrap timber

Jigsaw

Screws

Gold size

Transfer metal (silver) leaf

Cotton cloths

Scissors

Matt satin varnish

Day One

Step 1
Wearing heavy-duty gloves, apply paint and varnish stripper to the entire table using an old paintbrush. Leave until the paint begins to bubble and blister.

Step 2
Remove the stripper and paint from the flat areas with a flat paint scraper. Push the scraper away from you and the paint should come away easily.

Step 3
For the curved legs, remove the paint with a shaped paint scraper working in the same way.

Step 4
Work the stripper into awkward areas, such as the claw feet, using the nylon-bristled toothbrush, then rub off the paint with fine grade wire wool.

Step 5
Fill any cracks and holes using a neutral-coloured wood filler, smooth off the excess using the flat paint scraper.

1

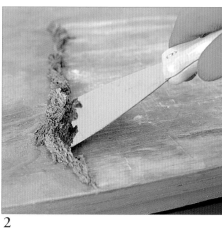

2

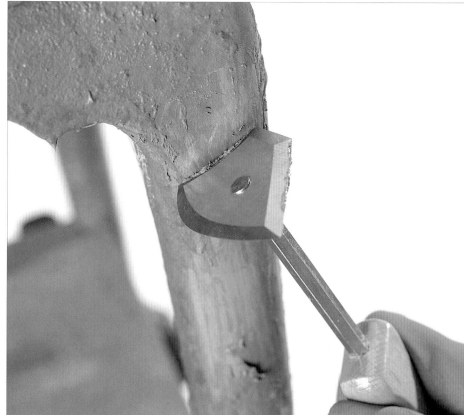

3

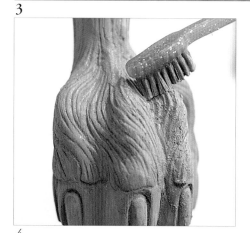

4

5

6

7

Step 6

Use an old paintbrush to force wood glue in between the layers of warped plywood on the tabletop. Protect the surface of the bedside table using off cuts of wood clamping them firmly together with G-cramps until the glue is dry.

Day Two

Step 7

Sand the table using an electric sander fitted with fine grade abrasive paper. If you do not have access to one, sand manually using the abrasive paper wrapped around a sanding block.

Step 8

Thin down the blue emulsion with a little water – this aids the paint application and avoids visible brushstrokes. Paint the entire table and leave to dry.

Step 9

Sand the painted surface with wet-and-dry paper wrapped around a sanding block (or just use fine grade abrasive paper) for a super-smooth surface. Apply another coat of paint.

8

9

Step 10

Measure the dimension of the missing drawer and cut a dummy drawer front from a piece of scrap timber using a jigsaw. Attach the wood in place using wood glue then screw in place.

Paint in the same colour as the rest of the table.

Step 11

Working in manageable sections, spread a thin layer of gold size onto the table using a clean paintbrush. Leave to dry for the manufacturers' recommended time – it should be just tacky to the touch before you apply the metal leaf.

10

Hints and Tips

When working with gilding materials, it is important to keep the working areas clean and free from dust. Any 'foreign bodies' that adhere to gold size will show up as surface faults when the leaf is applied and may cause it to tear when the item is in use. Keep spare metal leaf in case of repairs.

11

12

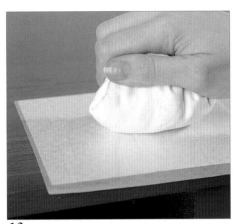

13

14

15

16

Step 12

When the gold size is tacky, carefully pick up a sheet of transfer leaf – handle it by the edges of the waxy backing paper. Apply it to the surface, lining up the square edge with the square edge of the table.

Step 13

Smooth down the transfer with a soft cloth, or clean fingertips, making sure that all edges are firmly stuck in place.

Step 14

Carefully peel away the backing paper starting with a corner to reveal the silver leaf. Line up a second square making sure that the edges butt neatly together. Press down and peel away the paper. Repeat until the whole table is covered.

On areas that do not need a whole sheet of metal leaf, cut the sheet to size. Use any leftover pieces to fill in bare patches where the leaf has torn or on curved areas, such as the legs.

Step 15

When dry, rub over the silver leaf very lightly with fine grade wire wool to expose the blue emulsion base coat in areas that would suffer from wear and tear.

Step 16

Cover the table with several coats of satin varnish sanding lightly between each coat.

Glossary

Abrasive paper

Abrasive paper
Available in various different grades (coarse, medium and fine) for use by hand or with electric sanders.

Acrylic varnish
A water-based varnish used to protect bare wood or a water-based paint finish.

Bradawl
A small tool with a sharp point used for making pilot holes for screws.

Bronze brush
A brush with many fine bronze bristles used for raising the grain of wood.

Electric sander

Cabinet scraper
A blade made of tempered steel with sharpened edges used for paint removal.

Contact adhesive
A powerful glue that forms a strong bond between two different surfaces.

Danish oil
A finishing oil for wood that nourishes the grain, gives a water-repellent finish and a subtle sheen.

Eggshell paint
The traditional trade name for a tough, durable paint with a mid-sheen used on wood or metal, available in water- or oil-based formulations.

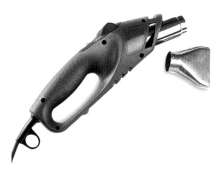

Hot-air gun

Emulsion paint
A general term for water-based paints used on walls and ceilings. It can also be used on woodwork but will require an additional protective top coat of varnish or wax.

Exterior oil-based varnish
Also known as polyurethane varnish, this is an oil-based protective coating for exterior woodwork and garden furniture. Water-soluble crackle varnish finishes should always be sealed with an oil-based varnish.

Filler
Available in paste, powder and flexible formulations, this is used for filling holes, cracks and imperfections in wood, plaster and masonry.

Foam applicator
A sponge-headed tool specially designed to avoid brush marks when applying woodstains and specialist paint finishes.

Glass etching spray
An aerosol spray that mimics the frosted look of etched mirror and glass but gives a semi-permanent finish.

Glazing beads
Strips of wooden moulding usually found on cabinet furniture, which hold glass panels in place.

Goggles
Protective eye wear used during many stripping techniques, but especially with a hot-air gun to shield the eyes from debris.

Gold size
Water- or oil-based glue specifically for adhering metal leaf to a surface.

Hot-air gun
An electric tool used for removing oil-based paints; it contains an element that heats up causing the paint to blister.

Iron paste/polish
A black paste applied to cast iron that when polished gives metal an attractive silvery graphite sheen.

Knotting solution
This liquid is applied to bare, resinous wood on the knots to prevent them bleeding through the painted finish.

Liming wax
A white wax finish, which is absorbed into the grain of porous woods like oak. Also used to highlight carvings and mouldings.

Loose metal leaf
Thin metal leaf, supplied loose in books, for gilding curved surfaces and mouldings.

Methylated spirits
A solvent used for thinning oil paints, cleaning brushes and removing shellac finishes, such as French polish.

Oil-based paint
A durable opaque paint that obscures the surface of the object.

Paintbrush
A brush for applying paint and varnish available in various sizes and qualities.

Paint scraper
This tool is available in a number of different shapes and is suitable for removing paint from different surfaces.

Paint stripper
Available in various forms, use these for varnished or painted surfaces that need to be taken back to the original surface.

Primer
This is used on bare wood, metal or plaster to seal the surface ready for finishing.

Putty (self-hardening)
A two-part putty, which when mixed together is self-hardening. Used to repair wooden mouldings and carvings.

PVA (Polyvinyl-Acetate) glue
A white, non-toxic, water-based wood glue that is absorbed into the wood forming a strong bond. Dries to a transparent finish.

Rust convertor/inhibitor
Often sold as a thick gel, this is used to convert existing rust back to bare metal and prevents new rust forming.

Sandblasting
A commercial process for stripping paint, rust and finishes from metal and brickwork.

Sanding blocks
Shaped pieces of cork or wood over which abrasive paper is wrapped, used for sanding rough surfaces. A flexible sanding block has abrasive paper permanently attached and is useful for curved areas.

Sugar soap
A commercial detergent for cleaning down old painted surfaces ready for stripping.

Tack rag
Cloth impregnated with oil, used for removing dust from a stripped item.

Transfer metal leaf
Supplied on wax backing paper, transfer leaf is good for gilding flat surfaces.

Knotting solution

Paintbrushes

Shaped paint scrapers

Wire brush and wire wool

Wood filler

Water-based paints

Any paint that is soluble in water, which includes emulsion, artists' acrylic paint, poster and powder paints. Well-used items will need a protective top coat of varnish.

Wet-and-dry paper

Common name for silicon-carbide paper – a fine grade, dark grey paper, used with water as a lubricant for sanding paint or finishing metal. It is also used to give a smooth finish to varnish, or distress a painted surface without causing scratches.

White spirit

Solvent for thinning oil-based paints, cleaning brushes and accidental splashes, and for removing wax and oil finishes.

Wire brush

Used to open up the grain on wood and clean flaky finishes from different surfaces.

Wire wool

This is available in various grades, from very fine (0000) to coarse (00). It can be used for cleaning wood, metal and glass, for applying wax, and for distressing painted surfaces. When using it with varnish and paint removers, always wear protective gloves.

Wood hardener

A commercial solution that strengthens and hardens decaying wood ready for filling and re-finishing.

Wood filler (or stopper)

Specially formulated filler for interior and exterior wood. Available in neutral and a variety of wood colours.

Wood restorer

Used to replenish oils on wood that has been treated with chemical stripper.

Suppliers

Black and Decker
210 Bath Road, Slough
Berkshire, SL1 3YD
Tel. 01753 574 277
Hot-air gun and multi-sander tools used on various projects.

Cornelissen and Son Ltd
105 Great Russell Street
London, WC1B 3RY
Tel. 020 7636 1045
Size and metal leaf used on mirror and bedside table projects.

Crown Paints
Crown Decorative Products Ltd
PO Box 37, Crown House

Hollins Road, Darwen
Lancashire, BB3 0BG
Tel. 01254 704 951
Crown crackle glaze used on garden bench project.

Cuprinol Ltd
Adderwell, Frome
Somerset, BA11 1NL
Tel. 01373 475 000
Cuprinol Advice Centre
Tel. 01373 475 000
Light oak wood dye used on chair project; rapid drying wood hardener, almond cream and soft willow colourwood used on garden bench project; white ash wood wash and crystal clear varnish used on door project.

Langlow
Palace Chemicals Ltd, PO Box 32
Ashridge Road, Chesham

Bucks, HP5 2QF
Tel. 01494 784 866
'Peel away' paint stripper used on fireplace project. Patent knotting used in Troubleshooting section.

Liberon
Mountfield Industrial Estate
New Romney
Kent, TN28 8XU
Tel. 01797 367 555
Liming wax, bronzing brush, and neutral wax on table project. Iron paste used on fireplace project.

The Milliput Co
Unit 8, The Marian
Dolgellau
Mid Wales, LL40 1UU
Tel. 01341 422 562
Self-hardening putty used on mirror project.

Index

This book is dedicated to Alex, not only for his input into its creation, but also for his general encouragement and support throughout.

Acknowledgements

Firstly, I would like to thank Natasha and the team at Merehurst for giving me this opportunity and for their support during the project.

Thank you to Graeme, David and all at Feelgood Studios, who produced excellent photography, as always; Caroline for her beautiful styling, hospitality and sense of humour; Shelley and Gabriella who were handy to have around; Black and Decker, and Cuprinol for supplying us with products; Fat Stan for making us all laugh; and last but not least, Alex for putting up with me.

First published in 2000 by Merehurst Limited,
Ferry House, 51–57 Lacy Road, London SW15 1PR

ISBN 1 85391 843 1

Commissioning Editor: Natasha Martyn-Johns
Design & Art Direction: Fay Singer
Project Editor: Sarah Wilde
Photographer: Graeme Ainscough
Stylist: Caroline Davis
Illustrations: Michael A. Hill
Production Manager: Lucy Byrne
Publishing Manager: Fia Fornari
CEO: Robert Oerton
Publisher: Catie Ziller
Group CEO/Publisher: Anne Wilson
Marketing & Sales Director: Kathryn Harvey
International Sales Director: Kevin Lagden

Colour separation by Colourscan, Singapore
Printed in Singapore by Tien Wah Press